Editor

Patricia Bahree M.A.

Managing Editor

Eric B. Inglefield B.A.

Production

Keith Ireland

ISBN 0 356 04972 8
© Macdonald & Co Ltd 1974

Printed in Great Britain by
Hazell Watson & Viney Ltd
Aylesbury, Bucks

MACDONALD'S
DISCOVERING THE EARTH

MACDONALD'S
DISCOVERING
THE EARTH

Roger Clare

CONTENTS

The changing Earth 84

Rocks and minerals 128

The Earth's story 144

People and the Earth 168

DISCOVERING THE EARTH

A train glides by on a monorail. The people inside are moving along quickly and in comfort. Through the windows they can see their city. There are tall skyscrapers and new buildings shaped like mushrooms. There are parks with trees and flowers. Is this what a city of the future will look like? It may be. The future depends on how we use the Earth now.

The Earth has a long history. But people have only been on it for a very short time. In that short time they have found out many things about the Earth. They have explored its oceans, mountains and air. They have learned to use the soil, the minerals and many of the other things the Earth provides. This book is about the Earth and some of the things that people have discovered about it.

Planet Mercury

Mercury was the messenger of the gods. The planet Mercury is named after him

Jupiter was the most powerful of the gods. The planet Jupiter is named after him

Planet Jupiter

MEET PLANET EARTH

What do you know about planet Earth? Probably quite a lot. You see it every day. You walk on it and dig into it and breathe its air.

Take a good look at the Earth around you. It may not look like a huge ball or sphere racing through space. But it is. Our Earth is one of nine planets that travel round the Sun. The Sun and these nine planets are called the Solar System. Our Solar System is just one of many in the Universe.

The Earth's neighbours

Can you name the planets in our Solar System? They are Mercury, Venus, Earth, Mars, Jupiter, Saturn, Uranus, Neptune and Pluto. Most of them are named after the gods and goddesses of people who lived long ago.

The planet Mercury is the smallest. It is named after the Roman god Mercury. He was the messenger of the gods.

The largest planet is Jupiter. It is named after Jupiter, the ruler of the gods.

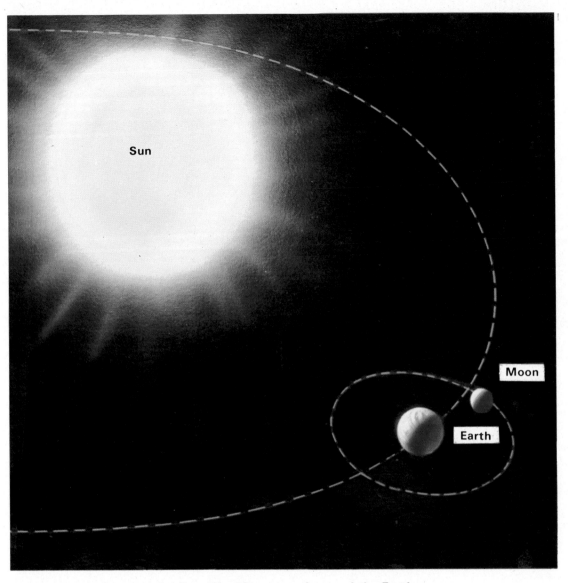

Sun

Moon

Earth

The Earth travels round the Sun. The Moon travels round the Earth

The Earth

The Earth is the fifth largest planet. It is the third from the Sun. The Earth has one Moon that travels round it. As the Earth circles the Sun, the Moon goes round the Earth. The Sun shines on both the Earth and the Moon.

Planet Earth

The Shape and Size of the Earth

Long ago people thought the world was flat. Sailors going on sea journeys were afraid they might fall off the edge. They thought that there were huge monsters in the oceans. One monster was called Balena. Sailors thought it had teeth and claws like a lion. It was probably a huge whale. Ziphius was another monster. It was supposed to have webbed feet and a beak.

Christopher Columbus braved the seas and monsters. He sailed across the Atlantic Ocean in 1492. Ferdinand Magellan sailed right round the world in 1522. He proved the world was not flat. But sailors still thought there were mermaids and serpents in the sea.

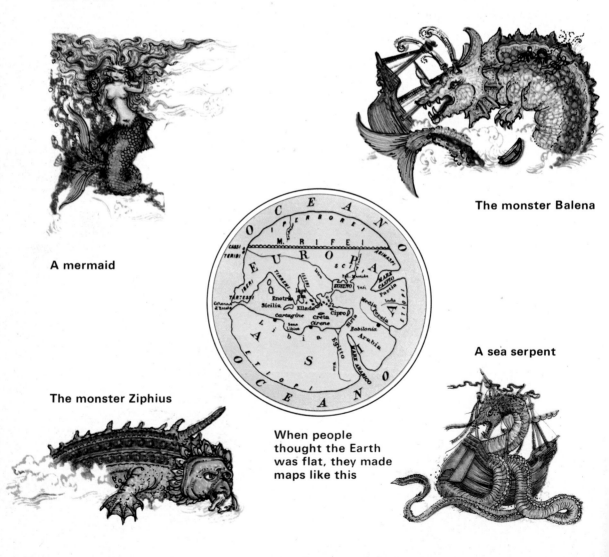

A mermaid

The monster Balena

The monster Ziphius

When people thought the Earth was flat, they made maps like this

A sea serpent

Is the Earth round?

We now know that the Earth is shaped like a round ball, called a sphere or a globe. But it is not perfectly round. Instruments on spacecraft have shown that it is a bit flat at the North Pole and South Pole. It also bulges a little at the middle.

The size of the Earth

On maps of the Earth, a line called the Equator marks the middle, half way between the Poles. If you go all the way round the Earth at the Equator, you will cover about 40 thousand kilometres. But if you could burrow straight through the Earth, you would have to make a tunnel about 13 thousand kilometres long to reach the other side.

This picture from space shows that the Earth is round

The spinning of the Earth causes day   **. . . and night**

The Movement of the Earth

Day and night

The Earth is like a giant spinning top that is tilted at an angle. It spins on an imaginary line that cuts through the Earth from the North Pole to the South Pole. This line is called the axis. As the Earth spins it is also moving round the Sun. This path around the Sun is called the orbit.

   The Sun only shines on half of the world at a time. Places facing the Sun have day. As the Earth spins toward the east, these places enter the area of shadow and it becomes night. Places where it was night move into the daylight.

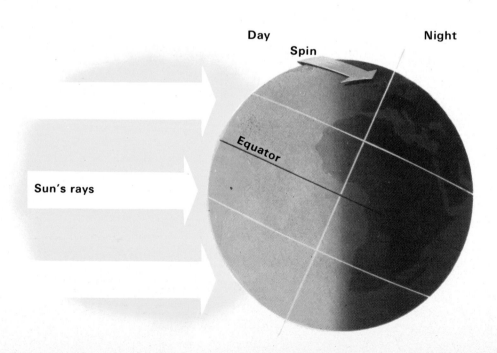

Day   Night

Spin

Equator

Sun's rays

This picture from space shows daytime over Africa

The Earth spins round once in 24 hours, but all places do not have 12 hours of day and 12 hours of night. Because the Earth is tilted, the land at the North and South Poles has 24 hours of daylight for some months of the year. In these months the Sun never sets.

What time is it now? That depends where you are. The world has been divided up into 24 time zones. Each of these zones has its own time.

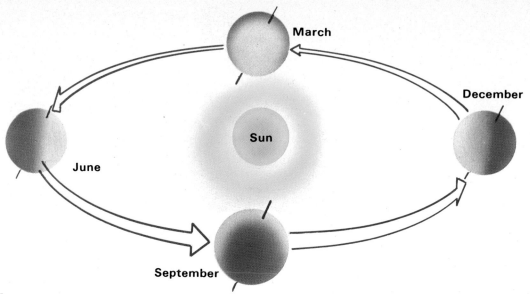

The seasons

The Earth travels round the Sun. It takes a bit more than a year, or 365 days, to go round the Sun. So every fourth year we add an extra day to the month of February to keep the calendar correct. That is a leap year.

The year is divided into seasons. For some months half the Earth leans towards the Sun. It has a summer season. The half leaning away is colder. Here it is winter. Between summer and winter, spring and autumn are the seasons.

Spring

Summer

Autumn

Winter

The Moon

The Earth has the Moon as a companion as it travels round the Sun. The Moon travels round the Earth and is carried along with it. It keeps to the same path, or orbit, round the Earth. The Moon takes 27 days and 8 hours to travel round the Earth. This is called a lunar month.

Full Moon

Quarter Moon

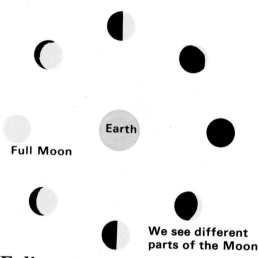

Full Moon

Earth

We see different parts of the Moon

The Full Moon

The Moon is a quarter of the size of the Earth. The Moon is covered with dust and pitted with craters. We can see it because it shines in the light of the Sun. At Full Moon we can see the whole side that is in sunlight. On some nights we can see only part of it. On other nights we cannot see the Moon at all.

Eclipses

Sometimes the Moon passes between the Sun and the Earth. It may then blot out the Sun's rays so that the day becomes dark. The Earth is then in the Moon's shadow. At other times the Earth passes between the Sun and the Moon. The curved shadows of the Earth may then pass across the Moon. These events are called eclipses.

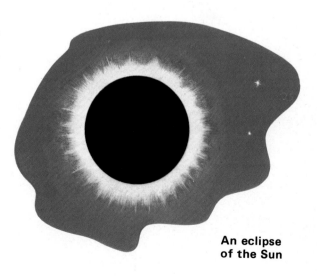

An eclipse of the Sun

The Earth's Big Pull

When you drop a piece of paper, why does it fall down and not up? Why do people and animals and houses stay on the world instead of drifting off into space? The answer to both questions is gravity. Gravity is a force which pulls things towards each other. Everything has gravity. The bigger a thing is, the stronger its pull.

The Earth's gravity is very strong. When you jump up, it pulls you down again. It keeps things from falling off the Earth. The Sun has gravity too. It keeps all the planets in orbit. Without it they would drift off into space.

What pulls the paper down? Gravity

Some racehorses are trained to jump as high as they can. But gravity brings them down again

A Hidden Force

The Earth's magnetic pull may help homing pigeons to find their way

A magnetic force we cannot see lies around the Earth. It is centred on the magnetic poles which are near the North and South Poles. People cannot feel the Earth's magnetic pull. But scientists think some birds may be able to. In cloudy or foggy weather, homing pigeons may use the Earth's magnetic force to find their way home from far away. In good weather they look for landmarks to guide them.

Compasses

Thousands of years ago, the Chinese found a kind of rock called lodestone that was magnetic. When allowed to swing freely, it pointed in a south-north direction. Lodestones were used to make the first compasses. A compass needle points to the magnetic poles. A compass can help you find which way you are going.

A compass needle points north

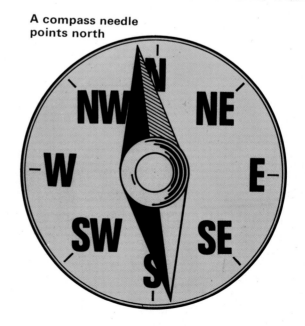

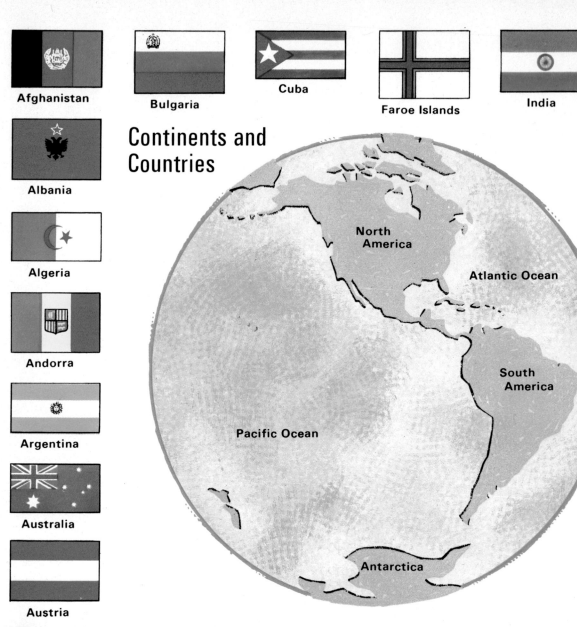

Afghanistan

Bulgaria

Cuba

Faroe Islands

India

Albania

Algeria

Andorra

Argentina

Australia

Austria

Belgium

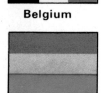

**Bolivia
Merchant Flag**

Some of the world's flags

Continents and Countries

North America

Atlantic Ocean

South America

Pacific Ocean

Antarctica

This half of the world is called the western hemisphere

Nearly three-quarters of the face of the Earth are covered by seas and oceans. Most of these are found south of the Equator. Most of the land is found north of the Equator. The land is formed mainly of large masses which are called continents. They are Europe, North America, South America, Africa, Asia, Australia and Antarctica. Asia is the largest continent and

North Korea

Morocco

Poland

South Africa

United Kingdom

United States

U.S.S.R.

Vatican City

**Venezuela
Merchant Flag**

North Vietnam

South Vietnam

Wales

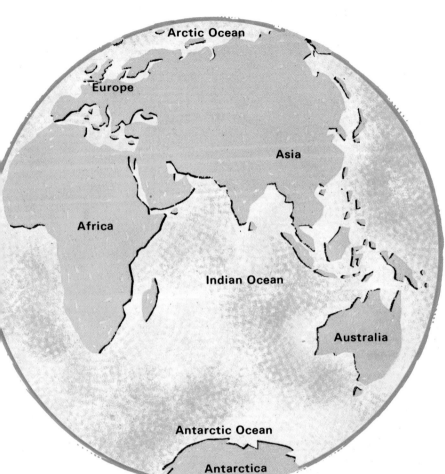

This half of the world is called the eastern hemisphere

Australia the smallest. Many smaller land areas, or islands, rise from the floors of the oceans.

People around the Earth have grouped together to form nations. They have divided up the land areas to make countries. Mountains and rivers sometimes mark the boundaries of these countries.

23

The Face of the Earth

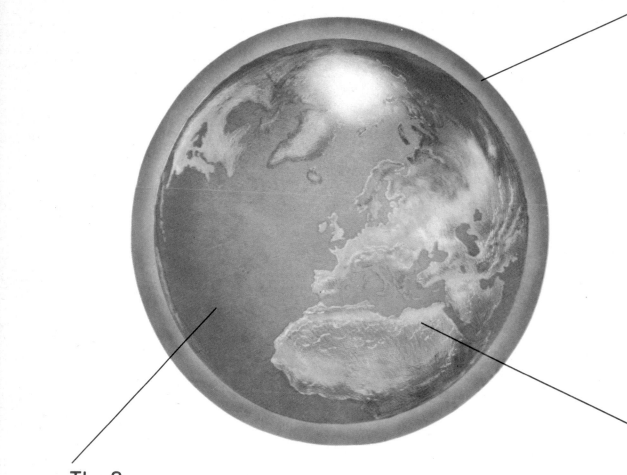

The Ocean

The Air

The Land

The land, the air and the oceans

Living things are found on the land, in the water and in the air that surround the Earth. Some creatures and plants live in only one of these three zones. For example, fishes live in the sea. Other creatures and plants may live in more than one zone. Birds live in the air, on the water and on land.

The Earth is covered by a crust of solid rock. But less than half of it is dry land. The rest is covered by water. Surrounding the planet is a thin layer of air called the atmosphere. Without this air there would be no life on Earth.

Read on to find out about the land, the air and the oceans.

THE LAND

Lands of Ice and Snow

Lands near the North and South Poles are cold because the Sun never rises high in the sky. For part of the year it does not rise at all. But for at least one day a year the Sun shines all day and night. That is why these lands are sometimes called the lands of the 'Midnight Sun'.

The area around the North Pole is the Arctic. The area around the South Pole is the Antarctic. The coldest parts of these lands are covered with very thick sheets of ice. The seas are frozen over most of the year. Scientists working there must have supplies brought in by special ships.

An icebreaker in the Antarctic

Huskies drag a dog
sleigh across the
Arctic ice

Exploring the cold lands

The first man to reach the
North Pole was an American
named Robert Peary. He
arrived there in 1909. He went
to Greenland and learned about
sledging from the Eskimos. He
built igloos from the snow
when he needed shelter and
wore Eskimo clothing.

A Norwegian explorer, Roald Amundsen, was the first man to
reach the South Pole. Amundsen used sleighs and huskies for
the journey. He arrived in 1911.

An Englishman, Robert Scott, set out for the South Pole with
a team of men at the same time. But they had a terrible journey
and arrived after Amundsen. On the return journey, Scott and
all his men died.

Today, Arctic and Antarctic travellers cross the ice in huge
snow tractors. These pull sleighs loaded with food, sleeping bags
and scientific equipment. Some tractors are so big that the men
can sleep in them.

Modern snow tractors

Seals

Summer in the cold lands

Not all of the Arctic is covered with ice all year. In summer the snow and ice melt away in many places. The ground is covered with a carpet of mosses and small flowers. These plants grow and flower quickly before winter sets in again.

Just below the surface the ground stays frozen all year. It never thaws out. In summer the melting snows cannot drain away. The land becomes marshy. In some places, mosquitoes swarm in the air.

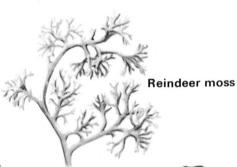

Reindeer moss

Sea bluebell

Arctic poppy

Visitors and herdsmen

Tourists often travel to the Antarctic to see seals and penguins. Sometimes they see beautiful birds.

Arctic reindeer move north for food in summer. The Lapps of Sweden follow the reindeer. They depend on them for much of their food and clothing. When they have returned south with the herds they spend the winter in comfortable modern homes.

Lapps follow the reindeer herds

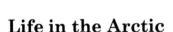
Polar bear

Life in the Arctic

Arctic animals are well suited to the cold. Seals spend much of their time in the sea. Because of their fur and their fat they do not feel the cold. Polar bears and Arctic foxes have thick furs that keep them warm. Some animals have coats that turn white in winter. This makes it difficult for their enemies to see them.

People hunt many Arctic animals for their furs. For many years the Eskimo people fished and hunted seal and caribou. But they only killed enough for their own food and clothing. There were many animals left. Today men with rifles have nearly wiped out some types of animals. They sell their furs for high prices.

Only a few Eskimos still hunt and fish. Most live in townships. They work at airports and for mining firms.

Arctic fox

The ptarmigan has brown feathers in summer and white in winter

Penguins

Forests

Some parts of the world are covered by great forests. The hot wet forests near the Equator have different plants and animals from those in the cooler parts of the world. There are two types of forest in the cooler lands. One of these types is the coniferous forest. The other is the deciduous forest.

This bird is a crossbill. It lives in coniferous forests

Coniferous forests

The coniferous forests are in the colder parts of the world. They stretch across the north of Canada and Russia. They grow on mountains in other countries, such as Chile and Switzerland. The name coniferous means that the trees have cones. Fir trees, pine and spruce are all coniferous trees. They can live in the cold and do not need much water. Their short branches slope down so they do not break under heavy snow.

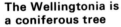

The Wellingtonia is a coniferous tree

A highway crossing a coniferous forest

Deciduous forests

Deciduous trees, such as oak and elm, have broad leaves and roots that spread wide. In winter they shed their leaves. Places where deciduous trees grow are warmer and wetter than those where coniferous trees grow.

Many kinds of animals live in deciduous woodlands. They make their homes in the trees and shrubs. Insects feed on the leaves and seeds.

Many deciduous forests have been cleared for farms

The oak is a deciduous tree

Some of the birds and small animals feed on the insects. Deciduous forests once covered large areas of South-East Australia, Europe, and the North-East of the United States. Now crops to feed thousands of people are grown in areas that were forest lands.

In North America, wheat is harvested on the prairies

Cool Grasslands

Vast grasslands called prairies once stretched across parts of the middle of North America. Similar grasslands are still found in other parts of the world. In Russia they are called the steppes and in Argentina the pampas.

Indians used to hunt bison on the American prairies. There were bison and pronghorn deer. Jackrabbits nibbled the grass. Prairie dogs and ground squirrels burrowed into the soil. Coyotes, wolves and golden eagles preyed on the smaller animals. These grasslands have changed over the years.

Sheep shearing

In Australia, the grasslands are used for sheep farming

Some hunters shot the bison from trains

Changes on the prairies

People from Europe settled in North America and caused most
of the changes in the prairies. The men hunted the bison with
guns. Some wanted the skins. Others killed them for sport.
Soon there were not many bison left.

The settlers who moved into these lands fought many wars
with the Indians. Finally the government placed the Indians in
special areas known as reservations. Here they had to find new
ways of living. The Indian lands were taken to make room for
farms. Railways were built to take the farm products away.
Cattle and sheep farmers moved into the areas. Then came
farmers who ploughed the land. Today, the prairies in the United
States look very different than they did one hundred years ago.

Cowboys round up cattle on the American
prairies

Hot Grasslands

Some of the hot parts of the world also have vast grasslands. These hot grasslands are called savannas. In some places they have burning deserts on one side and steaming forests on the other. Most hot grasslands are in Africa. There are also large grasslands in South America and Australia.

Grass and trees

Savanna grass is often thick and coarse. It grows so high that it is called elephant grass. Near the deserts, the savanna lands are dry much of the year. The grass withers and dries up. Near the forests, there are many bushes and trees among the grass. Some trees, such as the baobab, can live in the driest parts. The baobab stores water in its trunk.

Wild animals of the hot grasslands

Wildebeest

Zebra

Hippopotamus

Changes on the savannas

Long ago, forests grew in some areas where there are now grasslands. No one knows what caused the change. It may have been brought about by forest fires or by the people and animals of the grasslands.

Wild animals

Thousands of wild animals live in the savannas of Africa. Elephants and giraffes roam the land along with antelopes and zebra. Many savanna animals are plant eaters. But not all are. Sometimes the peace is shattered by a baboon's warning cries. Soon a cheetah or lion pounces on a fleeing animal.

Ostriches live on the African savanna

Elephant

Rhinoceros

ness

Deserts

Some parts of the world are hot dry places where little rain falls. These are the hot deserts. The largest is the Sahara in North Africa.

A Tuareg nomad

Desert people

Several groups of people live in the Sahara. Two of these are the Bedouins and Tuaregs. These people do not live in one place. They are nomads who travel across the desert. They live in tents made from goat skins or camel hair. To protect themselves from the hot sunshine and the cold nights they wear long flowing robes.

An oasis is a waterhole in the desert. Nomads move from one oasis to the next. Other people in the deserts live near an oasis. They use the water to farm the land and to grow crops such as dates.

Prickly cactus

Desert scenery

Strong winds often blow across deserts. They carry sand and blow it into piles called sand dunes. Sand dunes sometimes stretch across the deserts for hundreds of miles. But most deserts are huge areas of rock and stones rather than sand.

In sandy deserts, the wind blows the sand into dunes

A poisonous desert lizard

The saguaro cactus stores water in its its thick stem

Survival in the desert

People who live in the desert know its dangers and have learned how to survive. Travellers who do not know the desert may die of thirst.

Wilfred Thesiger was an Englishman who explored the Arabian Desert. Like the nomads he used a camel to carry his baggage. On his journey he had to cross miles of scorching sands and to face biting sandstorms. In these storms he would shelter behind his camel. He also had to be wary of one of the most dangerous creatures of the desert, the deadly scorpion.

Travellers today can cross deserts more easily in jeeps.

Desert plants

It is hard for desert plants to find enough water to live. Some plants have long roots. The roots go deep down into the ground to get water. The saguaro is a prickly cactus. It has roots which spread out just below the ground. When rain or dew falls the roots soak up as much water as possible. This is stored in the thick stem of the cactus.

Desert animals

Few plants and animals live in the desert because there is little water. But some plants and animals are suited to life in the desert.

The camel has double eyelids that keep the blowing sand out of its eyes. Pads on the camel's feet prevent it sinking in the sand. Fat in its hump enables it to go many days without food or water.

Many of the wild animals of the desert only come out at night when it is cool. Jerboas are desert animals that look like small rats. They live in cool underground burrows. The jerboa is hunted by other desert animals like the kit fox. But it can jump away quickly with its long back legs.

Rattlesnakes and lizards also live in the desert.

Kit fox

Rattlesnake

Jerboa

Jungles

In the lands near the Equator there are thick forests. They are called jungles or tropical rain forests. It is very hot all the time here. There is no summer or winter. There are heavy thunderstorms almost every day. The air is steamy. The rain and heat help plants to grow quickly all the year round. Many grow very large. The jungles are always green.

The River Amazon, in South America, flows through the world's greatest jungle.
Other great jungles are in Africa and Asia.

Some large areas in the jungles have been cleared to grow rubber trees, bananas, oil palms and pineapples. In many places the forests are being chopped down as roads are made. Life in the jungles is changing rapidly.

Jungle plants and animals

Viper

Layers of plants in the jungle

Jungle animals live at different heights

Jungle life

Plants grow at different heights in the jungle.
Tall trees form a canopy at the top which shuts
out the sunshine. Climbing plants grow up the
tree trunks to reach the sunlight. Some hang in
loops between the trees. Plants called epiphytes
have dangling roots which pick up water from
the air. Some orchids live high in trees where
they too can reach the light.

Each layer of the jungle provides food for
different animals. Smaller climbers, such as
the spider monkey, can reach the canopy.
Bigger animals find food on the forest floor.

Orchid

Parrot

Spider Monkey

41

Mountains

Edmund Hillary and
Norgay Tenzing

Everest 8,848 metres
(Asia)

Aconcagua 6,960
(South America)

McKinley 6,193
(North America)

Kilimanjaro 5,895
(Africa)

El'brus 5,642
(Europe)

Cook 3,764
(Australia)

The highest
mountain in
each continent

Mountains are found in many parts of the
world. They rise above the deserts and the
jungles and form islands in the sea. Some
mountains stand alone. Others are in long rows
called mountain ranges.

Climbing the highest mountain

Mountaineers try to climb to the top of the
highest peaks. The highest mountain in the
world is Mount Everest. It is in the Himalaya
mountains. The Himalayas stretch across parts
of India, China and Nepal.

The first men to reach the top of Mount
Everest were Sir Edmund Hillary from New
Zealand and Norgay Tenzing from Tibet. They
planted a flag and Tenzing left some sweets
and biscuits as a religious offering.

Mountain passes

The high peaks of mountains form a barrier which it is difficult to cross. Places where people can cross through the mountains are called passes. Farmers use these passes to move their sheep and cows from one pasture to another. People from many lands have come to India through the Khyber Pass in the Himalayas.

Today mountains are becoming easier to cross. Trains have been made that can climb steep slopes. Tunnels have been cut through some mountains for cars.

Crossing a mountain pass in the Himalayas with a herd of yaks

Eagle

Mountain goat

Bighorn sheep

Ibex

Chamois

Mountain weather

As you go up a mountain, the weather changes. The higher you go, the colder it gets. High in the mountains, there is a lot of rain and snow. If you climb high enough, you will reach the snow line. Above this point, it is so cold that snow covers the ground all year.

Mountain animals

Near the snow line the ground is steep and rocky. Only hardy animals can survive here. They are suited to the conditions. Animals such as the mountain goat, the ibex and the chamois have special hooves. These help them climb steep rocks without falling. Their thick coats keep them warm. Eagles soar above in search of prey.

These animals are suited to life in the mountains

Mountain plants

Plants grow in zones on mountains. As you go higher, the plants of one zone disappear and new ones are found. Mountains in warm, wet parts of the world may have forests at the bottom. The trees here lose their leaves in winter. They are called deciduous trees. Higher up there are evergreen trees such as firs and pines. These strong trees can stand the cold. Their branches slope and bend under the weight of the snow.

Still higher it is too cold for trees to grow. Above this level, called the tree line, only shrubs and wild flowers can grow. Among the bare rocks of the mountain peaks only mosses and small plants called lichens can survive.

Edelweiss

Snow buttercup

Snow and ice

Tree line

Coniferous forest

Deciduous forest

Different kinds of plants grow at different heights in the mountains

45

Rivers

Rivers drain away the rain that falls on the land. They take it down to the sea. Rivers have been highways along which people have travelled since they first made boats. They have been used to carry goods for trade. Often they have been used to explore new lands. Many famous explorers followed the rivers to see what lay in the heart of Africa. Two of the best-known explorers were Stanley and Livingstone.

The longest river in each continent

Africa

South America

North America

Asia

Australia

Europe

Nile 6,670 kilometres

Amazon 6,276

Mississippi-Missouri 5,954

Ob'-Irtysh 5,471

Murray-Darling 3,717

Volga 3,684

The longest rivers

The Nile is the longest river in the world. It flows more than 6,600 kilometres from the lakes of East Africa down to the Mediterranean Sea. The River Amazon is in South America. It has many other rivers flowing into it. They drain a very large area. In Australia the River Darling flows down from the eastern mountains. It joins the River Murray. Together the Murray-Darling rivers are nearly 3,700 kilometres long. What is the longest river in your country?

River life

The kinds of fish in a river depend on where the river is in the world. There are also different kinds of fish in different parts of the river. In English rivers tiny sticklebacks and minnows live where the water flows quite fast. Large perch and pike live in the slow waters.

Many types of birds and animals live beside rivers. They feed off river plants, insects and fish. Some animals, such as otters, swim and catch fish and frogs.

People often live by rivers. They use the water for their crops and industries and in their homes. At the waterside they load goods on and off boats. Many of the world's greatest cities are built by rivers. Many grew where the first bridges were built.

Catfish

Minnow

Pike

Perch

Stickleback

Flounder

There are many river fish. Some are big and others tiny

Many large cities have grown up along rivers

Lakes

Lakes are made when water fills big hollows in the ground. The largest lake in the world is so large it is called an inland sea. This is the Caspian Sea in the south of Russia. Lakes are often found high in mountains. Lake Titicaca in the Andes mountains is one of the highest lakes in the world. Lake Baikal in Siberia is the deepest lake. It is over two thousand metres deep.

Lakes were made in different ways. Some were made long ago by ice sheets which scraped out holes in the ground. Some lakes were formed in the hollow tops of old volcanoes. Sometimes a lake formed when a river was blocked by lava from a volcano or by land sliding from a hill.

Lakes scraped out by ice sheets

A lake in the crater of an old volcano

A lake forms when lava blocks a river

A lake forms when a landslide dams a river

Birds, frogs and toads live around lakes

Lake life

Many plants and animals live in lakes. Others live along the shores. The tall grass that grows around lakes makes a good home for birds. Herons live near lakes. They use their long beaks to grab fish from the water. Grebes dive for fish. Frogs and toads also live near the water. They feed on insects.

Some lakes do not have much life. One lake is called the Dead Sea because it is too salty for animals to live in. In dry lands shallow lakes form after rain storms. These lakes soon dry up in the hot sunshine.

Many other animals and plants live under the water

THE AIR

Birds fly naturally

A thin layer of air covers the whole Earth. We call this layer the atmosphere. Near the ground there is plenty of air. As we go higher there is less and less air.

Exploring the atmosphere

Men have always wanted to explore the air and space beyond. Long ago they dreamed of flying like birds. Some fixed wings to their arms and jumped from high places. But nobody ever managed to fly. Men first flew by using balloons filled with hot air.

People have tried to fly like birds

The first aeroplane with an engine was built by the Wright brothers. How does an aeroplane fly? As the aeroplane moves forward air moves under the wing and pushes it up. The air rushing over the curved top of the wing sucks the wing up. Aeroplanes which fly faster and higher are being made now. They have powerful jet engines.

When rockets first went into space many new things were found. One discovery was the Van Allen Belt. Here there are rays which are dangerous to space travellers. This area stretches far into space.

The first flight was by balloon. Now airliners take people round the world

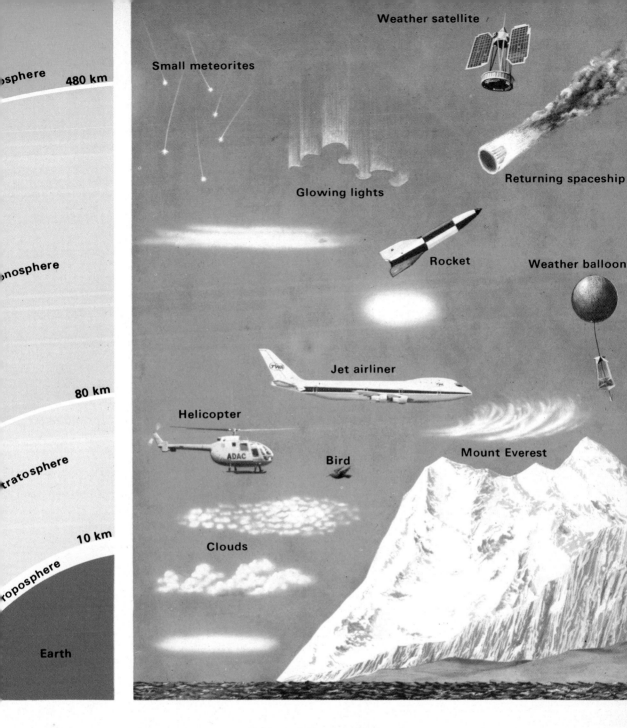

osphere   480 km

Small meteorites

Weather satellite

Glowing lights

Returning spaceship

nosphere

Rocket

Weather balloon

80 km

Jet airliner

tratosphere

Helicopter

ADAC

Bird

Mount Everest

10 km

Clouds

roposphere

Earth

The layers of the atmosphere

The picture on the right shows some of the things in the atmosphere up to 1,000 kilometres above the Earth

The layers of the atmosphere

Nearly all the air that we breathe is in a layer close to the Earth. Here, too, clouds are found. Above this layer is the stratosphere, where the air is very thin. Higher still is the ionosphere. Here the atmosphere is electrified and there are streams of glowing lights.

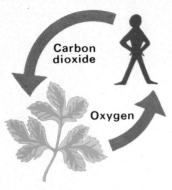

Plants give out oxygen which people need. People breathe out carbon dioxide which plants need

Why the atmosphere is important

There would be no life on Earth without the atmosphere. Most of the air is made of the gas nitrogen. It also has other gases. People, animals and plants need these to live.

When people and animals breathe in they use the oxygen in the air. They breathe out another gas called carbon dioxide. This gas is needed by plants. Plants then give out oxygen. Neither animals nor plants can live at great heights, because there is not enough air.

When the Sun shines on the Earth the air lets the light pass through. But the air protects us from the very hot rays from the Sun. At night, the air acts like a blanket and stops too much heat escaping.

The air also acts like a filter. It takes out the dangerous ultra-violet rays that would kill all living things on the Earth. The atmosphere is like a huge glasshouse protecting the Earth.

Birds use the air to fly

Plants and animals cannot live on high mountain tops. This is partly because the air is thin there

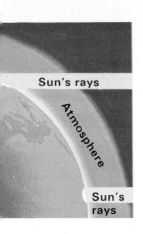

The atmosphere filters out dangerous rays

The atmosphere traps the Sun's heat like a greenhouse

Telephone calls and television programmes are sent from one country to another by communications satellites. Signals are sent through the atmosphere to the satellites. The satellites pass them back through the atmosphere to some other part of the world

Satellites

A cyclist riding along slowly on a calm day can hardly feel the air. If he goes quickly the air pushes against him and slows him down. This is called drag. Near the Earth the atmosphere is quite thick, or dense. This is where the air causes most drag.

Scientists have to use powerful rockets to launch satellites above the dense part of the atmosphere. Otherwise the air will slow the rockets down and they will fall back to Earth.

Some satellites are made to pass on telephone messages and television programmes. These are called communications satellites. They are so high up that a satellite above the Atlantic Ocean can send messages between America and Europe.

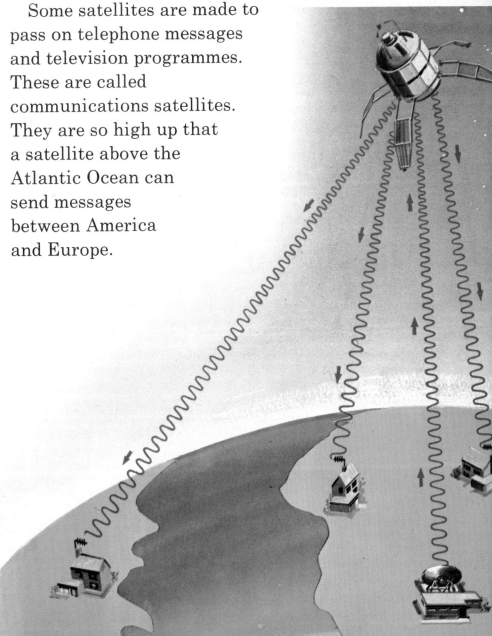

What Makes the Wind Blow?

If you hold your hands over a radiator, you can feel hot air rising. The air is heated by the radiator. The hot air rises because it is lighter than the cold air round it. As the hot air rises, cooler air moves in to take its place. The same sort of thing happens in the atmosphere. The moving warm and cool air is the wind blowing across the Earth.

Sea breezes

On the sea-shore, you have probably felt a cool breeze blowing in from the water. This happens because heat from the Sun warms the land faster than the sea. The land heats the air above it, just like the radiator. The warm air rises and cool breezes from the sea move in beneath it. You cannot see the warm air rising above the land. But you can see the seagulls gliding high in the sky as they 'ride' on the rising warm air.

At night, the land cools faster than the sea. The warm air above the water rises. The wind changes direction and blows out to sea.

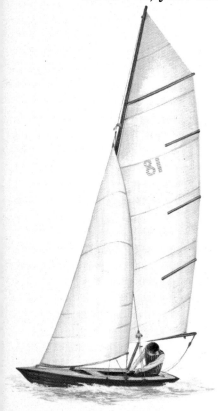

Sea breezes are caused by moving warm and cool air. Small yachts use breezes to move across the water

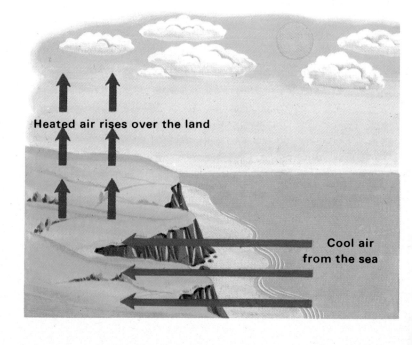

Heated air rises over the land

Cool air from the sea

54

Winds of the world

Some winds blow a long way across the Earth. The Sun beating down at the Equator warms the Earth. The air is heated and it rises high in the atmosphere. It cools and finally sinks back to the Earth's surface. Here it spreads out as winds. As they blow across the Earth, they gradually change direction. This is because the Earth is spinning round.

Some of the world's winds have names. The Trade Winds were used by the trading ships of long ago.

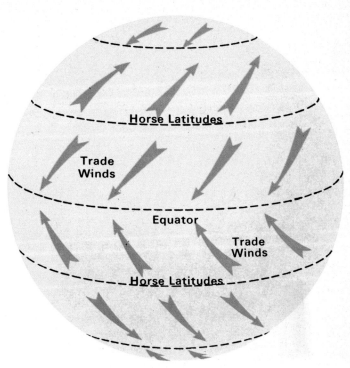

This map shows the winds of the world. The calmer places called the Horse Latitudes have an interesting history. They often slowed down trading ships carrying horses. If food and water ran short, the horses were dumped overboard. That is how the Horse Latitudes got their name

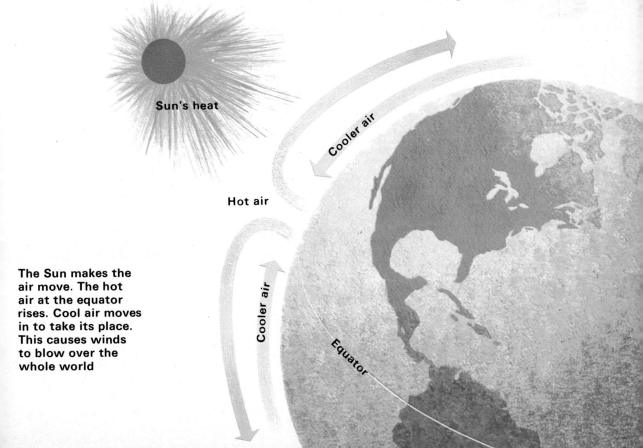

The Sun makes the air move. The hot air at the equator rises. Cool air moves in to take its place. This causes winds to blow over the whole world

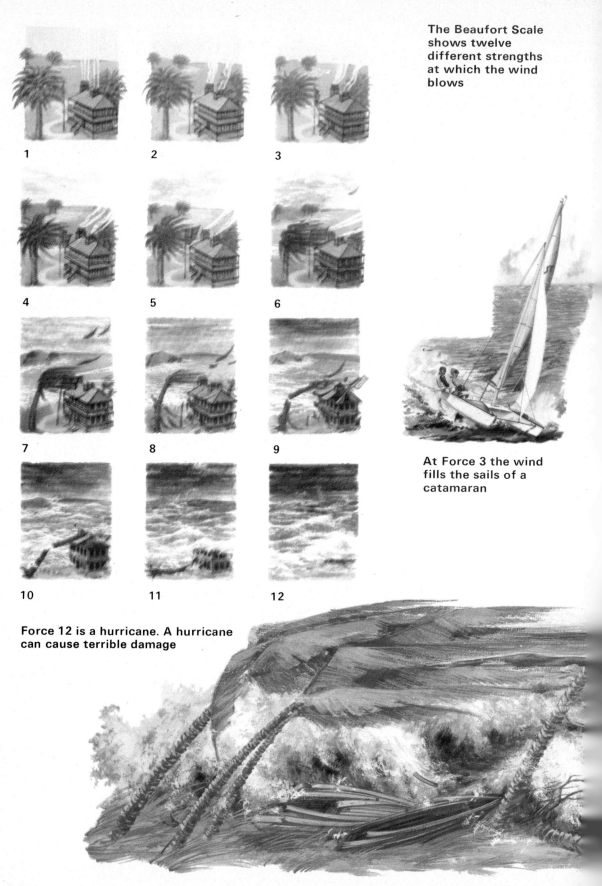

The Beaufort Scale shows twelve different strengths at which the wind blows

1

2

3

4

5

6

7

8

9

10

11

12

At Force 3 the wind fills the sails of a catamaran

Force 12 is a hurricane. A hurricane can cause terrible damage

How Strong is the Wind?

On some days there is no wind. But on other days, you may be blown off your feet by a strong gale. A wind may be light or it may be strong. Weathermen use a scale to describe the speed, or force, of winds. This scale was worked out by an admiral, Sir Francis Beaufort, to warn sailors more than a hundred years ago. It is called the Beaufort Scale. It was based on the wind at sea. Since then, the scale has been changed so that it can be used on land.

   The scale number goes up as the wind gets stronger. At Force 1 the wind is a light breeze. You can hardly feel it. At Force 4 there is a moderate wind. Dust and loose paper are blown about. Small branches sway on the trees. Force 8 is a gale. Force 10 is a strong gale, with winds travelling at over ninety kilometres an hour. The most powerful wind of all is Force 12. This is a hurricane. It can uproot trees and destroy houses. At sea, it causes huge waves which may wash in and flood the land.

Tornadoes and Hurricanes

A tornado is a violent wind. It is a great column of whirling air rising from the ground and travelling very fast. As the tornado moves, it sucks up everything in its path. Dust, fences, roofs and even cars are lifted high into the air and dropped back to earth.

Tornadoes blow over very hot, flat land. The air above the land is hot and rises very fast into the sky, whirling round and round.

Luckily, tornadoes do not last long. When they move from flat land the spiral of air usually breaks up and the tornado dies.

How a tornado moves

A tornado is shaped like a funnel

58

Hurricanes are violent storms. They happen over warm seas where the air is hot and moist. As the warm air rises it circles round and round. There are roaring winds. Thick clouds form and torrents of rain pour down. The centre, or 'eye', of the hurricane is calm.

The islands in the Caribbean Sea are often in the path of hurricanes heading towards the southern coast of the United States. Because they cause so much damage and loss of life they are carefully tracked to warn people of their approach. Aircraft, radar and spacecraft are used to find hurricanes. Experts are looking for ways to stop hurricanes forming.

Aircraft are used to track hurricanes and tornadoes

A hurricane on a radar screen

Clouds

Jet aeroplanes fly high in the sky where the air is thinner and they can travel more quickly. They fly above the layer of the atmosphere where nearly all the weather forms.

Jet planes fly above the clouds

Different types of clouds

The passengers in a jet aeroplane can look down on the tops of the clouds. The tops shine brightly in the sunlight. When people on Earth look up they see the bottoms of the clouds, which are often dark and gloomy.

Some clouds look like grey blankets across the sky. These are stratus clouds. Sometimes the stratus clouds are made of rounded masses joined together. These are strato-cumulus clouds. Separate, fluffy, white clouds are cumulus clouds. Sometimes these clouds tower upwards and have flat spreading tops shaped like an anvil. They are then called cumulo-nimbus clouds. These clouds often bring thunderstorms. Highest of all are wispy clouds of ice called cirrus clouds.

Some different kinds of clouds

Cirrus

Cumulus

Strato-cumulus

Cumulo-nimbus

Stratus

Alto-cumulus

Dew is caused by the condensation of water from the air

Dew, Mist and Fog

If you go out early in the morning you may find the grass covered with tiny drops of water. This is called dew. It is formed when the air cools during the night. Warm air can hold more water vapour than cold air. When warm air gets colder, some of the vapour turns back into water. This is called condensation.

On very cold nights the dew may freeze. Everything is then covered by a white frost. Condensation also causes mist and fog. Mist is made of millions of tiny drops of water. It forms when warm moist air near the ground is cooled. If the mist gets thick it becomes fog.

Fog is caused by condensation

Rain and Snow

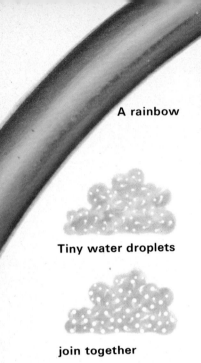

A rainbow

Tiny water droplets

join together

and fall as rain

Why it rains

Clouds and rain are formed when air rises and cools. Air that has passed over the sea is warm and moist. As it rises the water vapour in it cools and condenses. The tiny droplets of water that form make up clouds. As the air gets cooler still, more and more droplets are formed. They join together until they become so big that the air cannot support them. Then they fall as rain.

It often rains in the mountains. This is because moving air is forced to rise over them. As it does so, it cools and rain falls.

You can sometimes see a rainbow when the Sun shines on the rain. The raindrops split the sunlight into different colours.

Rain falls

Clouds fo

A

Water flows back into the sea

Why snow falls

In the colder parts of the world snow often falls in winter. Children then enjoy throwing snowballs or making snowmen. If you catch snowflakes and look at them before they melt, you will see that they are all different. Snowflakes have many different sizes and patterns, but they always have six sides.

Sometimes it is so cold in the clouds that tiny ice crystals form in them. As the crystals grow heavier, they fall through the clouds. Water droplets freeze onto these crystals and form feathery snowflakes.

If the air below the clouds is very cold, the crystals fall as snow. If the air is warm, they melt and fall as rain. Sometimes snowflakes only partly melt as they fall. They fall as sleet.

Snow never falls in most parts of the world. But in other places it falls all the year. These parts are around the North and South Poles and high in the mountains.

Throwing snowballs

Snow crystals have six sides

Thunder and Lightning

Lightning flashes and thunder crashes in a thunderstorm. Lightning is an electric spark. Sometimes the sparks are passing from cloud to cloud. At other times they are passing between the cloud and the ground. Thunder is the noise lightning makes as it travels through the air. You hear the thunder after the flash of lightning because sound travels more slowly than light. You can work out how far away a thunderstorm is. It takes the noise of thunder three seconds to travel a kilometre after the lightning flashes.

What causes thunderstorms? Great masses of warm and cold air move through the atmosphere. Where they meet the weather changes. The cold air pushes beneath the warm air. Clouds form and rain falls. Sometimes there are thunderstorms.

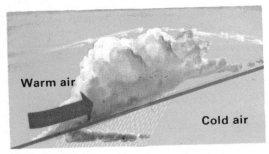

When warm air rises over cold air, heavy rain usually falls

Lightning flashes during a thunderstorm

Thunderstorms happen when hot moist air rises and cools quickly. Dark clouds form and big drops of rain fall. Only the largest raindrops fall because the air is rising so quickly that smaller drops are carried upwards.

As these drops go up they may freeze. As they come down they are covered with a layer of water. Then they are carried upwards again and the layer of water freezes. This goes on until they are so heavy they fall as hailstones. You can see these layers if you cut open a hailstone.

Hailstones cut in half show layers of ice

Cold air

Warm air

When hot air rises high in the sky, thunder clouds form and rain falls

Weather Watching

People called meteorologists, or weathermen, use instruments to measure and to record the weather. They can find out from other meteorologists all over the world what the weather is in different places. They use this information to tell, or forecast, what the weather will be.

Sunshine recorder

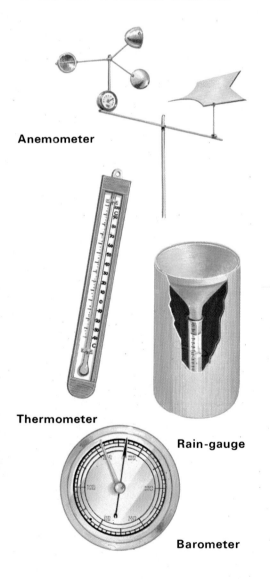

Anemometer

Thermometer

Rain-gauge

Barometer

A weather station

Many kinds of instruments are used to measure the weather. They are kept at a weather station. Some stations are at airports. Others are on ships.

An anemometer is used to measure the speed and direction of the wind. It has cups which spin round in the wind.

Thermometers are used to measure how hot the air is. A barometer is used to measure the pressure of the air.

Rainfall is collected through a funnel and measured in a rain-gauge. Sunshine recorders burn a track on a piece of paper that shows how many hours the Sun has shone.

Weather satellite

Tracking station

Instruments in the sky

Weathermen use balloons filled with gas to carry instruments high in the sky. The instruments send information about the weather to them by radio.

Weather satellites also send back information. This is used to forecast the weather several months ahead. Satellites also help weathermen to discover when hurricanes are beginning to form.

A weather balloon with instruments

Forecasting the weather

Weathermen make charts to show what the weather is like. They also prepare simpler charts for television. These are shown as part of the weather forecast. They have special symbols on them to show rain, fog and the speed of the wind. There is a symbol for every part of the weather. The lines show where the air pressure is high,

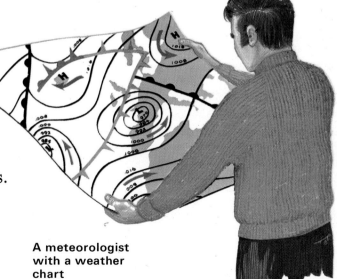

bringing calm weather, or where it is low, bringing storms. Lines are also drawn to mark the edges of air masses. These show the way the weather is moving.

A meteorologist with a weather chart

THE OCEANS

Alexander the Great is lowered into the sea

Halley's diving bell

Exploring the Depths

People have been sailing over the oceans for thousands of years. But few have actually been to the bottom to have a look around. No one knows who was the first deep-sea diver. It may have been Alexander the Great. Stories say that over two thousand years ago Alexander went down into the ocean in a barrel. He wanted to see the strange animals that lived at the bottom of the sea.

In 1690 Edmund Halley built one of the first diving bells. It could hold more than one diver. Barrels of air were lowered down to them.

Over a hundred years later the first diving suits were made. Then air could be pumped to divers from a ship.

Land

The ocean floor has high mountains and deep chasms

Chasm

The ocean floor

Even with diving suits, divers could not go down to the deepest parts of the oceans. Other ways had to be found to map the ocean floor. For a time, scientists tried lowering lines overboard to measure the ocean depths. Today scientists work on special ships. They use shock waves to make maps of the ocean floor.

Scientists have found that there are broad plains, great mountains and deep chasms on the ocean floor. They have discovered a long chain of mountains running down the centre of the Atlantic Ocean. Many islands in the ocean are the tops of these mountains.

This record of the ups and downs under the sea was made by an echo sounder. It uses shock waves

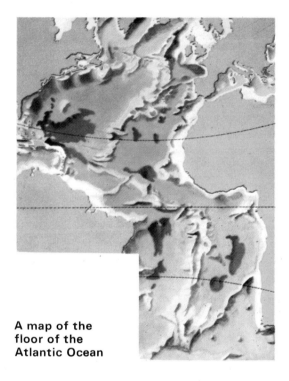

A map of the floor of the Atlantic Ocean

Island

Land

Mountains

Slope

Deep-sea plain

A modern deep sea diving suit

Aqualung

Cousteau with his aqualung

Divers today

Divers in diving suits can stay underwater a long time. But they cannot go far from the ship that is pumping air to them.

A Frenchman, Jacques Cousteau, invented the aqualung. Aqualungs are bottles of air which a diver carries on his back. He is free to explore coral reefs and old ship-wrecks. Diving with aqualungs has become a popular sport. But divers with aqualungs can only go down about 50 metres.

To go deeper, divers need strong diving suits to protect them against the great pressure of the water.

Bathyscaphes

A deep-sea ship or bathyscaphe, called the Trieste went down into a great chasm in the Pacific Ocean. This chasm is known as the Marianas Trench. Here, more than nine kilometres down, it is very dark. Strong lights shone from the bathyscaphe. The scientists were surprised when they saw strange fish. They had thought no fish could live at these depths.

A bathyscaphe is made of very strong metal. This stops it being crushed by the weight of the water above it.

Before the first bathyscaphes were built, scientists were lowered in huge metal spheres.

600 metres
Bathyspheres can go this deep

3000 metres

Deep-sea cameras can go this deep

6000 metres

A bathyscaphe can go this deep

9000 metres

The ocean depths

The bathyscaphe 'Trieste'

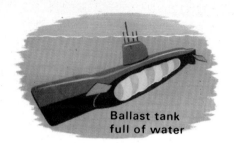

Ballast tank
full of water

Submarine dives

Submarine stays level underwater

Ballast tank
filling with air

Submarine surfaces

Submarines

Submarines are ships that travel beneath the sea. The first submarine was made from wood five hundred years ago.

The most modern submarines are driven by nuclear power. They can stay below the surface for many weeks.

How does a submarine work?

There are ballast tanks on each side of a submarine. When these tanks are filled with sea water, the submarine gets heavy and sinks. Different tanks are used to stop the submarine from sinking too far and to keep it level. The submarine rises to the surface again by blowing the water out of its ballast tanks.

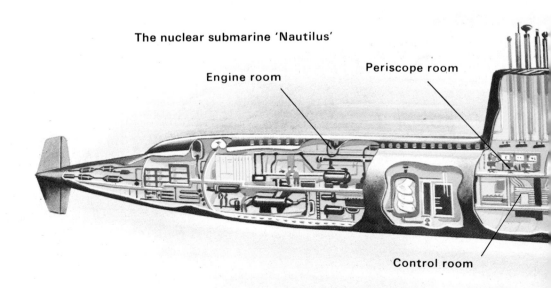

The nuclear submarine 'Nautilus'

Engine room

Periscope room

Control room

Garage for
diving saucer

Starfish House

Living Beneath the Sea

The underwater village 'Conshelf'

One day people may be able to build towns beneath the sea. Underwater laboratories have been built for divers to live in. These undersea explorers are called aquanauts. They need a special supply of nitrogen, oxygen and helium to breathe. Without this, they would receive very painful injuries when they came back to the surface.

The famous diver Jacques Cousteau built an underwater village. It was called Conshelf. Conshelf was made up of three houses built on the floor of the Red Sea. One of the houses was a garage for a diving saucer. This saucer was used to take divers down to three hundred metres. The aquanauts lived in the largest building. It was called Starfish House.

The aquanauts collected fish and rocks. They made films of the plants and fish. They proved that men and women could live and work under the sea for several weeks.

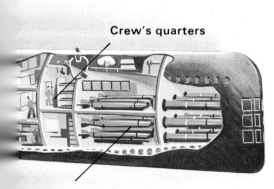
Crew's quarters

Torpedoes

The Tides

Twice each day in most parts of the world, the level of the sea rises. The water slowly creeps up and covers a large part of the sand or pebbles on the sea-shore. In some places it beats against the cliffs. This is called the high tide.

Twice each day the sea level falls. The rocks and sand are uncovered. We can walk along places that were under water a few hours before. This is called the low tide.

Low tide

What causes the tides?

Sailors once believed tides were made by a huge monster in the oceans. The real cause is almost as surprising. Tides are caused by the Sun and Moon pulling the oceans toward them.

The Sun and Moon move in a regular pattern. They cause two big bulges of water to form and sweep around the world. When the Sun and Moon are both on the same side of the Earth, they have the strongest pull and the tides are highest.

Tides and sea life

When the tide goes out, it leaves seaweed, small fish and other kinds of sea life behind. Some small sea animals bury themselves in the sand and wait for the tide to come in.

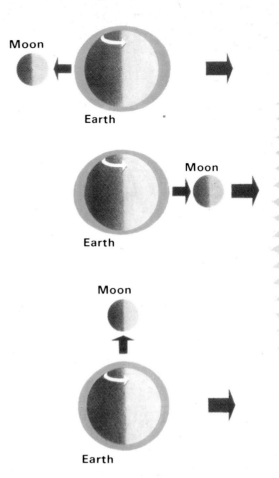

The pull of the Sun and Moon causes the tides. When they pull together, the tides are highest

When the tide goes out all kinds of sea plants and animals are left behind

Ocean Currents

If you put a message in a bottle and put it in the ocean, it might be found in some far off land. How would it get there? The ocean currents would carry it. The currents are moving streams of water in the oceans. The currents move in great circular patterns, round the oceans.

Currents of sea water move because the oceans near the Equator are warmed by the Sun more than those near the Poles. The currents begin as warm and cold waters mix.

Winds blowing across the world also carry along the waters. The spin of the Earth causes currents to change direction slightly.

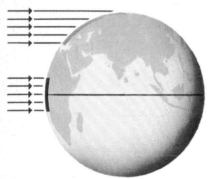

1. The Sun warms the Earth most near the Equator

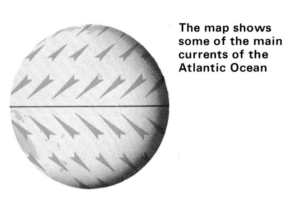

2. Winds blow because air moves between the cooler and warmer parts of the Earth

3. The winds blow over the oceans and help to cause currents

The map shows some of the main currents of the Atlantic Ocean

Cold current ➝
Warm current ➝

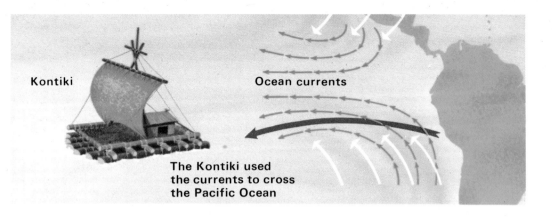

Kontiki

Ocean currents

The Kontiki used
the currents to cross
the Pacific Ocean

Deep-sea currents

Deep below the surface, currents of cold water move slowly
across the ocean floors. Scientists are still trying to find out
what causes these deep-sea currents.

Exploring the currents

Thor Heyerdahl is a famous Norwegian scientist. He showed that
people may have used currents to cross the oceans thousands of
years ago. He built a raft of balsa wood just like those built
long ago. It was named Kontiki. Heyerdahl and a few crew
members sailed the Kontiki 6,800 kilometres across the Pacific
Ocean. He left from Peru in South America and arrived at the
Polynesian Islands. His trip showed that the islands might have
been settled by Indians from South America.

Using the currents

Scientists think some fish may
use the ocean currents when
they migrate. Eels lay their
eggs in the Atlantic Ocean
near the West Indies. The
newly hatched eels float with
the currents to the shores of
Europe. It takes them two
years to get there. Then they
swim up the rivers.

Eel

Waves

Sometimes the wind causes high waves

If you watch a beach ball floating on the sea on a calm day you can see it rising up and down on gentle waves. When the weather is stormy the waves are much higher. Some waves are more than a hundred feet high. They can wreck ships at sea. They can also cause great damage along the coast.

How waves are made

Most waves are caused by the wind. It makes the water move round in a circle. As the wind blows harder over the sea, the waves get bigger. They become longer and deeper. Some waves are caused by earthquakes. Gentle earthquakes often form waves round the coast of Japan. Big earthquakes form huge waves called tsunamis. Sometimes these waves drown many people.

This Japanese print shows waves caused by an earthquake

Waves rise and fall in a circular movement

Sea horses

Life in the Sea

Many interesting types of fish live in the oceans. The colours and markings on many fish are beautiful. They are also useful. Flatfish change colour to match their surroundings. This makes it hard for their enemies to see them. The butterfly fish has a spot that looks like an eye. This confuses its enemies who do not know if it is coming or going.

Some fish use poison or electricity to protect themselves. There are over 50 kinds of poisonous fish. Electric fish stun their prey with an electric shock.

There are many strange fish. The porcupine fish blows itself up. Its spines stand out. This makes it difficult for other fish to swallow it. Sea horses do not look like other fish. They have strange heads. They often hook themselves to coral with their long tails.

Butterfly fish

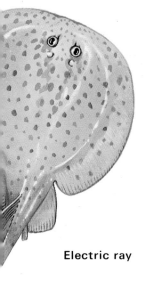

Electric ray

This flatfish has changed colour to match a chessboard

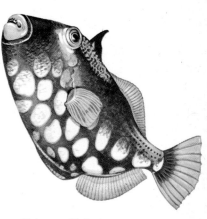

Trigger fish

Pipe fish

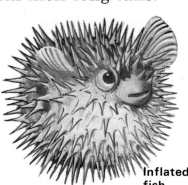

Inflated porcupine fish

79

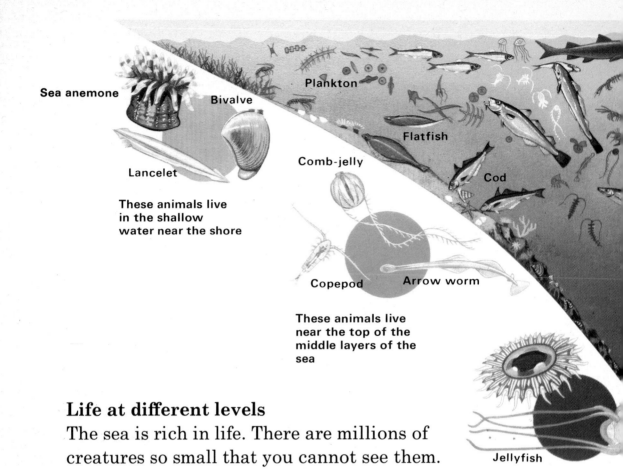

Sea anemone

Bivalve

Lancelet

Plankton

Flatfish

Comb-jelly

Cod

Copepod

Arrow worm

Jellyfish

These animals live
in the shallow
water near the shore

These animals live
near the top of the
middle layers of the
sea

These animals live
near the bottom of
the middle layers
of the sea

Life at different levels

The sea is rich in life. There are millions of
creatures so small that you cannot see them.
There are blue whales over 30 metres long
that weigh more than 135 tonnes. There are
giant worms and animals that bloom like
flowers.

Millions of tiny plants and animals called plankton live near
the top of the sea. The tiny plants use sunlight to make food.
They are eaten by the tiny animals. These plants and animals
are eaten by larger sea animals.

Around the shores, in the shallow water, seaweeds grow.
They need sunlight to live. As the water gets deeper the
sunlight gets weaker until no weeds can grow. Many animals
live among the seaweeds. There are sponges, starfishes and
sea anemones. Lobsters and crabs live here too.

Most plants and animals live in the warm sunlit surface
layers of the oceans. In the deepest parts, it is very dark and
cold. Strange gulper eels and angler fish live here.

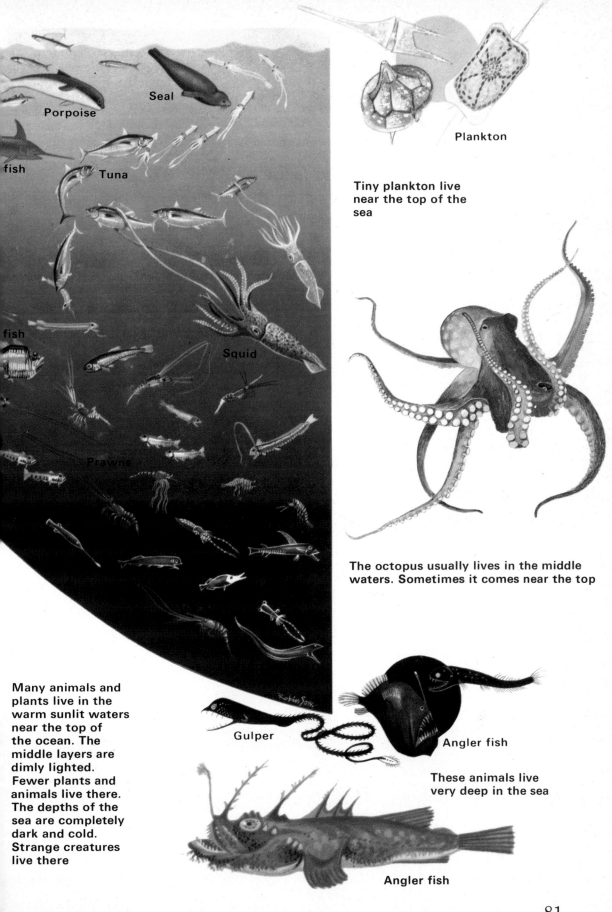

Porpoise

Seal

fish

Tuna

fish

Squid

Prawns

Plankton

Tiny plankton live near the top of the sea

The octopus usually lives in the middle waters. Sometimes it comes near the top

Many animals and plants live in the warm sunlit waters near the top of the ocean. The middle layers are dimly lighted. Fewer plants and animals live there. The depths of the sea are completely dark and cold. Strange creatures live there

Gulper

Angler fish

These animals live very deep in the sea

Angler fish

81

Coral Islands

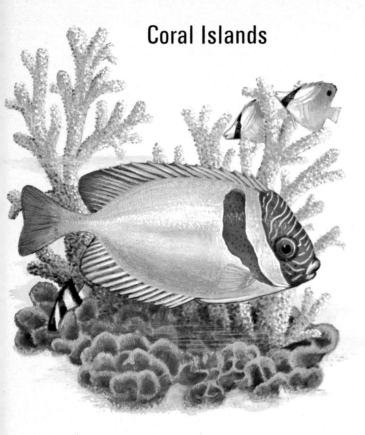

Many tropical fish live in coral reefs

Corals are small jelly-like ocean animals. They are usually brightly coloured. Some are red or purple. Others are yellow or green. They have tiny tentacles with which they catch plankton, their food.

Most corals live in places where the seas are warm, clean and shallow. They grow together in giant groups.

Each coral makes a cup of limestone around its soft body for protection. When the animal dies, its cup is left behind. New corals grow on top of the old ones like branches or fans.

Coral reefs

Very slowly a tall wall of coral builds up from the bottom of the sea. It is called a coral reef. Many fish shelter in the reefs and in the seaweed growing on them. Tropical fish that live in coral reefs are often bright red, pink or blue. They blend well with the bright colours of the coral reef.

A coral reef

Reefs and islands

The reefs grow upwards from the seabed until they are just beneath the surface of the sea. Ships are sometimes wrecked on coral reefs. Some reefs grow a long way from the shore. These are barrier reefs.

Other reefs grow close to the shore. These are called fringing reefs. Some fringing reefs form on the tops of underwater mountains. When the sea level falls the top of the reef stands above the water. A circle of coral islands is formed called an atoll.

Scientists have drilled through Eniwetok atoll in the Pacific Ocean. They found that the coral was 1,600 metres thick. Coral can only live in shallow water, so the scientists know these waters were shallow at one time.

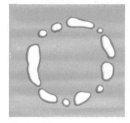

A circle of coral islands is called an atoll

Top view

Side view

An atoll

THE CHANGING EARTH

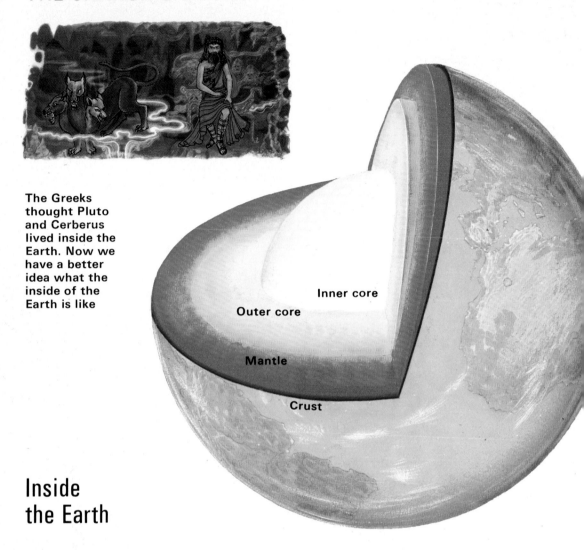

The Greeks thought Pluto and Cerberus lived inside the Earth. Now we have a better idea what the inside of the Earth is like

Inner core

Outer core

Mantle

Crust

Inside the Earth

What is inside the Earth? People have been trying to find out for thousands of years. The ancient Greeks thought the god Pluto lived there. He had a fierce dog with three heads called Cerberus. Pluto and Cerberus guarded the land of the dead. They also kept watch over valuable gems found in the Earth.

The ancient Romans thought the god Vulcan lived in the Earth inside a volcano. He was blacksmith to the gods. Sometimes the volcano rumbled and clouds of black smoke filled the air. The Romans thought Vulcan was lighting his fires.

People in Japan once thought there was a huge spider inside the Earth. This spider was said to cause earthquakes.

Finding out about the Earth

Today we know much more about the inside of the Earth. Volcanoes and earthquakes puzzled people long ago. But they have helped scientists find out what the inside of the Earth is really like.

The layers of the Earth

The outside skin of rocks on which we live is called the Earth's crust. The thickest part of the crust is about 50 kilometres. In some places beneath the ocean the crust is as little as five to eight kilometres thick. Compared with other layers, this is very thin. In relation to its size, an apple has a thicker skin than the Earth.

The layer beneath the crust is the mantle. It is nearly three thousand kilometres thick. Scientists have tried to drill through the crust to get samples of the mantle, but they have not been successful.

The centre of the Earth is called the core. The outer core is so hot that the rocks are in a molten, or melted, state. Scientists think the inner core is made of solid nickel and iron.

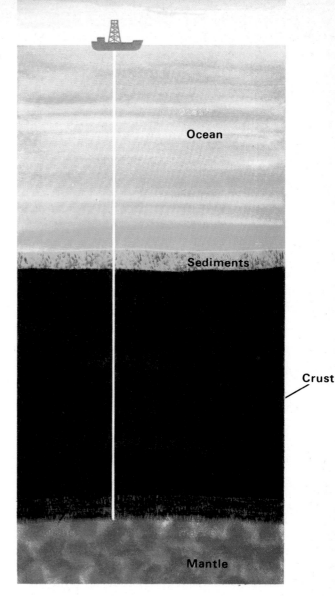

Ocean

Sediments

Crust

Mantle

Scientists tried to drill through the crust but were not successful

Some coal miners work 900 metres down. But they are still in the Earth's crust

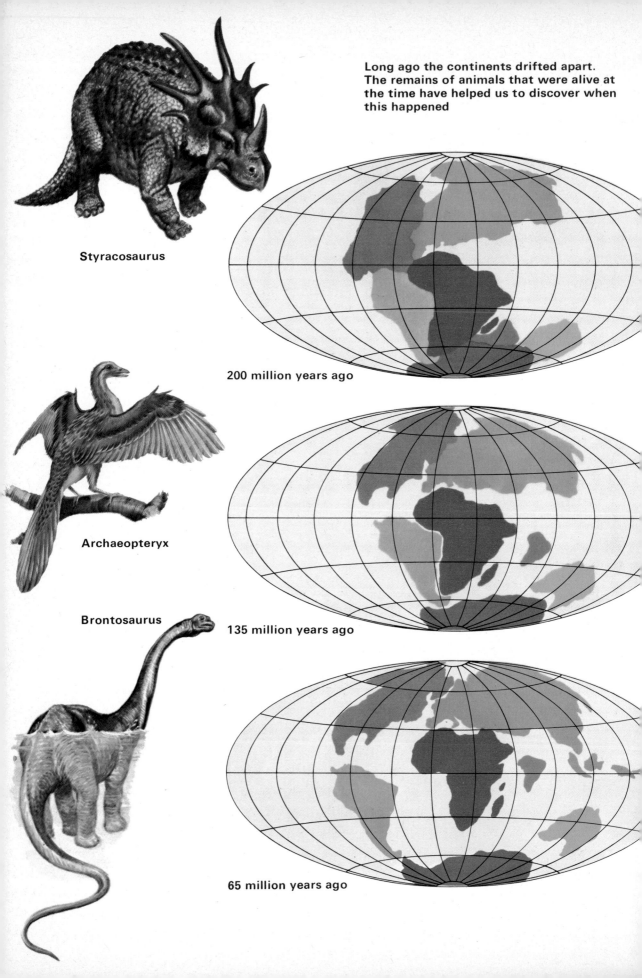

Long ago the continents drifted apart.
The remains of animals that were alive at
the time have helped us to discover when
this happened

Styracosaurus

Archaeopteryx

Brontosaurus

200 million years ago

135 million years ago

65 million years ago

Drifting Continents

Look at the map below. Think of the land as pieces of a jigsaw puzzle. Can you find any pieces that fit together? Africa and South America are the easiest to match. The rest of the continents can also be joined up. Scientists think they can be fitted together because they were once one large continent. They call this continent Pangaea. It probably began to break up and drift apart about 200 million years ago.

Other clues also show the continents were once joined. Dinosaur skeletons have been found on several continents. The dinosaurs could not have crossed the ocean. But they could have travelled across land when the continents were joined.

There is coal under snow and ice near the South Pole. We know that coal was formed in hot forests. The land may have drifted from a warm part of the world to the cold polar area.

Tyrannosaurus

An early mammal

Corythosaurus

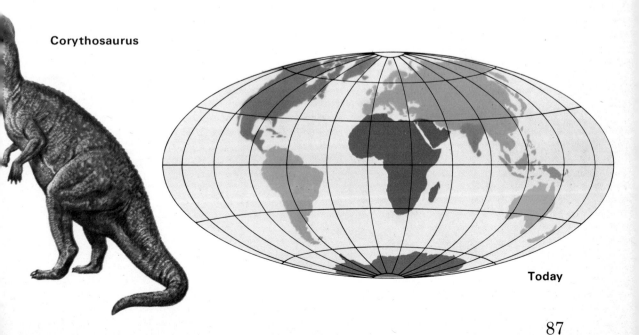

Today

Continents moving apart

The continents are still moving across the face of the world.
They are travelling very, very slowly. The crust of the Earth
is cracked into pieces like the shell of a broken egg. These
pieces are called plates. Terrific forces deep in the Earth are
moving these plates along.

One of these cracks is along the middle of the Atlantic Ocean.
The rocks in the mantle deep beneath this crack are not solid.
They rise up and force their way through the crack. Then they

Liquid rocks rise up along the crack in the Earth's crust beneath the Atlantic Ocean

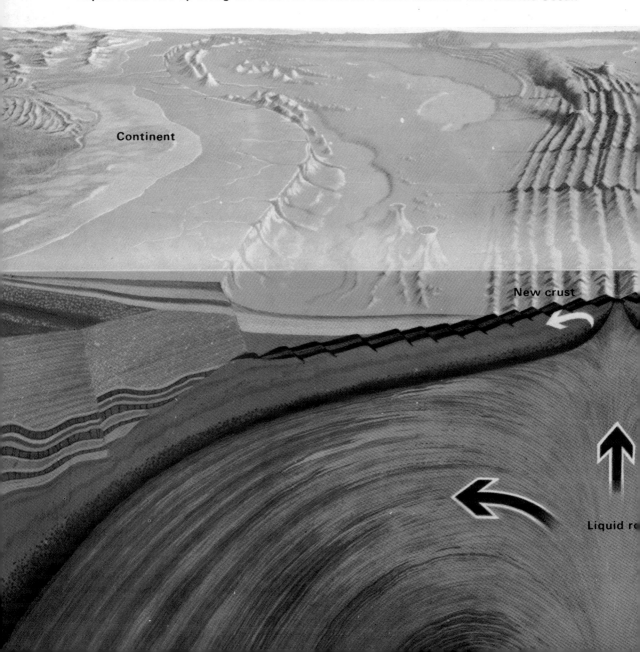

Continent

New crust

Liquid r

cool and become solid. As they become solid they push apart the plates of the Earth's crust on each side. A new crust is being formed. Gradually the Atlantic is becoming wider. North America is moving 25 millimetres further away from Europe every year.

As the plates of the Earth's crust move about they grind against each other. They cause earthquakes as they move. They push the rocks up to make mountains. In some places, the plates are even pushed under each other. Where this happens the rocks go back down deep into the Earth. Here they melt again.

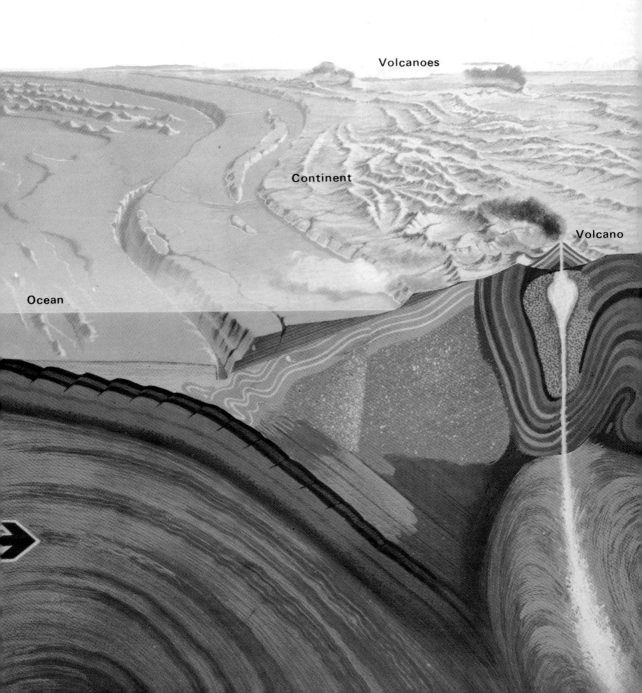

Volcanoes

Continent

Volcano

Ocean

The Himalaya mountains were pushed up as India collided with Asia

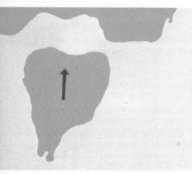

India moves north

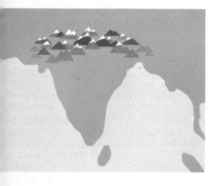

India collides
with Asia

Mountains rise up
where one plate of
the Earth's crust is
pushed against
another

Pushing up the Mountains

Seashells have been found in the rocks high in the Himalaya mountains. At some time these rocks must have been beneath the sea.

The continents have been moving about for millions of years. Sometimes they have collided. When they collide they push up layers of rock to form mountains.

India was once many kilometres away from Asia. Then India began to move towards Asia. As it got closer, the rocks in the sea between India and Asia were pushed up for thousands of metres. That is how seashells got up in the mountains. India is still moving and pushing the Himalayas a little higher every year.

Mountains

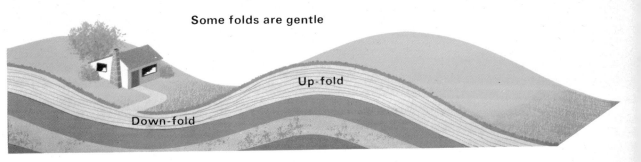
Some folds are gentle

Up-fold

Down-fold

Folds

When you look at cliffs you can often see folds in the rocks. Folds are places where the Earth's movements have bent the rocks. Some folds are very gentle. They were formed when there was not much force. When the fold is arched up it is called an up-fold, or an anticline. A down-fold is called a syncline.

Sometimes there is a lot of force from one direction. The rocks may fold right over.

Rocks fold over and break

Faults

As the rocks move they split and break. These breaks are called faults. Sometimes great blocks of rocks are pushed up along these faults. They may be so high that they form mountains. In other parts great blocks drop down. These form rift valleys. The Great Rift Valley runs for hundreds of kilometres through East Africa.

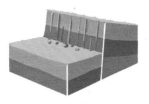
Blocks of land move up and down along faults

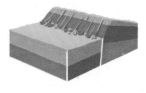
The edges are worn away very slowly

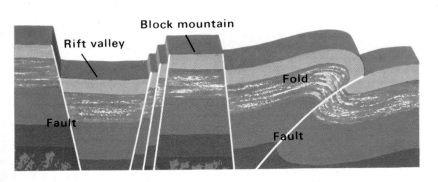
Block mountain

Rift valley

Fold

Fault

Fault

Many different shapes in the land are made by folds and faults

Poseidon was said to cause earthquakes

Earthquakes

What causes an earthquake?

The ancient Greeks believed that their god Poseidon caused earthquakes. They sometimes pictured him as a bull. As he stamped on the ground the Earth shook.

Scientists today know that the land we live on is always moving. Earthquakes are caused when one piece of land moves against another. This puts a great strain on the rocks. Suddenly the rocks give way. They usually move along a crack, or fault. As they slip and break, the surrounding land shakes and trembles. Slight earthquakes are only recorded by delicate instruments. In a stronger earthquake, people will wake and church bells will ring. In a very strong earthquake, the ground breaks and twists. Buildings may fall down and whole cities may be destroyed. Often many people are killed or hurt.

Thousands of small earthquakes happen everyday. Big ones cause a lot of damage

Great forces push the crust of the Earth.
Suddenly the rocks move

Earthquake waves
can twist a fence

Strange events

Some strange things happen during earthquakes. Fences, roads
and railways may be twisted into wavy lines. Sometimes the
Earth shifts several metres along a fault. Then fences and roads
are broken apart. The gap between the two parts shows how far
the Earth has moved.

In some earthquakes the ground opens up and then closes again.
In an earthquake in California the ground opened and swallowed
a cow. When it closed again only the cow's tail was sticking out.

People in Japan are warned to stay indoors during an
earthquake. They are told not to try to escape by car. An
earthquake can damage the roads and cause accidents.

During an
earthquake the
Earth breaks and
moves along a fault.
Part of a road may
end up higher than
the rest

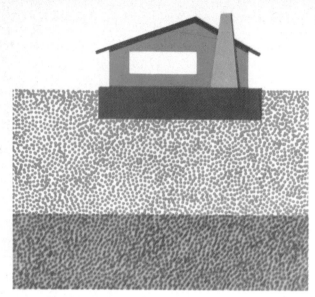

Some houses are built on sand

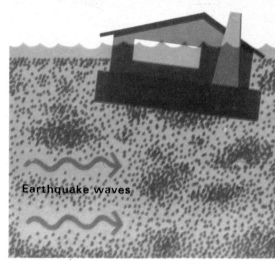

Earthquake waves

These houses may sink in an earthquake

Tall buildings can be made that will not tumble during an earthquake

Forecasting earthquakes

It is hard to tell *when* an earthquake will happen. It is easier to tell *where*. Earthquakes tend to happen where the plates of the Earth are pushing against one another or sliding alongside each other. Sometimes huge faults, or cracks, develop. When the pressure becomes great enough, it is likely the Earth will suddenly move along these faults.

Buildings for earthquakes

In places where earthquakes often happen, buildings are built in special ways. Tokyo is a city that has many earthquakes. So buildings are put up that do not fall down easily if the ground shakes.

In sandy places, earthquakes can cause buildings to sink into the ground. Earthquakes shake up the water in sand. The sand becomes quicksand. Buildings then sink into it and become flooded.

An old earthquake recorder

The Chinese knew how to record earthquakes two thousand years ago. One of their instruments had a ring of eight dragons' heads around the top. Each held a bronze ball. If the Earth shook enough, the balls would fall into a toad's mouth. The balls that fell showed the direction of the earthquake.

An early Chinese earthquake recorder

Recording earthquakes today

Earthquakes send out different types of shock waves. There are push waves like the movement of a punch-ball. Shake waves rock from side to side. Long waves are like the ripples made when you throw a stone into a pond. Scientists study these waves to find out where the earthquake began.

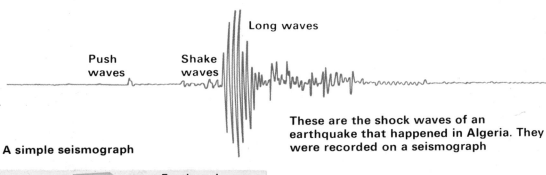

Push waves   Shake waves   Long waves

These are the shock waves of an earthquake that happened in Algeria. They were recorded on a seismograph

A simple seismograph

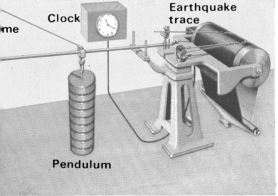

Clock   Earthquake trace   Pendulum

The seismograph

There are about a million earthquakes every year. A delicate instrument called a seismograph records even the gentlest earthquake. It traces all the shock waves onto a graph.

Volcanoes

When Mount Vesuvius erupted, the city of Pompeii was buried in hot ash

About two thousand years ago the volcano Vesuvius erupted in Italy. There was a great explosion. Hot gases, dust and ash were thrown in the air. The nearby town of Pompeii was buried in the ash and many people died. Pompeii has now been unearthed. We can see what the homes were like. Plaster has been poured into the holes where people were buried and casts made of their bodies.

Volcanoes erupt when molten rock is forced upwards from deep inside the Earth. This molten rock pours out as lava. It cools into a solid rock. Sometimes ash, lava and steam are thrown high in the air. At other times hot gases may shoot out down the side of the volcano.

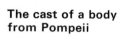

The cast of a body from Pompeii

96

An exploding volcano throws ash and lava high into the air. Lava pours down the sides

Not all volcanoes are alike. Some erupt mildly

In others, a lava plug blocks the vent. Ashes, steam, hot gases and lava shoot out of the side of the volcano

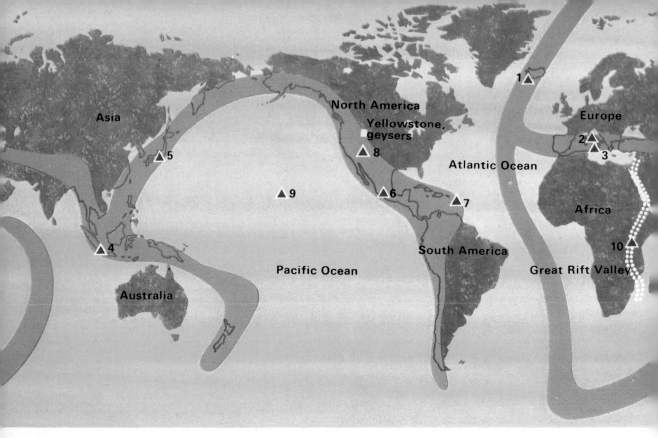

Where volcanoes are found

There are more than four hundred volcanoes in the world today. Most are found in a belt round the Pacific Ocean. There are so many that this belt is called the Great Ring of Fire. Nearly all volcanoes are found where the crust of the Earth is cracked and weak.

The band marks the volcano belt. Some volcanoes are shown
1. Surtsey
2. Vesuvius
3. Stromboli
4. Krakatoa
5. Fuji
6. Parícutin
7. Pelée
8. Sunset
9. Mauna Loa
10. Kilimanjaro

SOME VOLCANIC DISASTERS		
Year	Volcano	Number of People Killed
79	Vesuvius, Italy	About 2,000 in Pompeii and Herculaneum
1669	Etna, Italy	20,000
1815	Tamboro, Indonesia	12,000
1883	Krakatoa, Indonesia	36,000
1902	Pelée, Martinique	30,000

A terrible disaster

In 1902, Mount Pelée, on the island of Martinique, showed signs that it was about to erupt. But people in the nearby port of St Pierre took little notice. Suddenly the side of the volcano burst open. A cloud of hot ash, steam and gas shot down the mountain side, and 30 thousand people died.

Surtsey rises from
the sea bed

A new vent opens

Lava flows out and
the new island
grows even larger

An island is born

Some volcanoes are beneath the sea. A few years ago, a fisherman
to the south of Iceland saw a glow beneath the waves. To his
surprise, the sea was hot. A few months later, a new island
appeared there. It was a volcano. As it erupted great pieces of
lava were flung through the air. Lava poured into the sea and
made it boil. At last, the volcano died down. Birds and plants
began to live on the island. The people of Iceland called the new
island Surtsey, after a giant in an old legend.

Hot water from the ground

In some parts of the world steam and gases hiss from the ground.
There are springs and jets of hot water and pools of boiling mud.
All these are caused because there are molten rocks not far
below the ground. Rain seeping down boils and shoots high in
the air. This boiling fountain is called a geyser.

Hot mud

Hot spring

Geyser

Cones and craters

Volcanoes are shaped like cones. Some have steep cones made of cinders and lava. Fuji Yama, in Japan, is one of these volcanoes. Others have flatter cones made from runny lava. Mauna Loa in Hawaii is one of these.

At the top of a volcano is a huge hole. This is the crater where the lava pours out. When a volcano stops erupting for a long time the crater may fill with water and form a lake. Crater Lake, in the United States, is one of these lakes. In the middle of the lake is Wizard Island. It was made when the volcano erupted again and formed a small, new cone.

Many old volcanoes no longer erupt. Sometimes the crater fills up with water to form a lake

Crater lake

The remains of a volcano

Edinburgh Castle, in Scotland, stands guard on a hard, high rock above the city. This rock was once the inside of a volcano.

The volcano died long ago. Some of the molten rock became solid inside the cone. Rain, wind, snow and ice then wore away the soft cinders and ashes of the cone. The hard rock at the centre has taken longer to wear away. This hard rock is called a neck. It still stands, with its castle on top. But one day, it too will be completely worn away.

A volcano wears away slowly. After many years it may look like a low hill

Edinburgh Castle

Wearing Away the Land

All the rocks that you can see are slowly being broken up by the weather. Buildings are also being attacked. The stone from which they are made becomes pitted and pieces flake away. This is called weathering.

The weather wears away rocks. Sometimes odd shapes are made

Water fills a crack

The water freezes. The crack grows

The rock breaks

The work of ice and rain

When it rains water may seep into small cracks in the rocks. If the water freezes it turns into ice. As it does so, it takes up more space, or expands. Every time this happens the cracks are pushed wider and wider apart. At last they split and the rock breaks up.

Sometimes the rain beats down so heavily that it wears away soft earth and clay. Strange pillars with huge stones perched on top are left. These stones have protected the soft clay beneath from the rain.

These pillars were made by rain beating on on the rocks

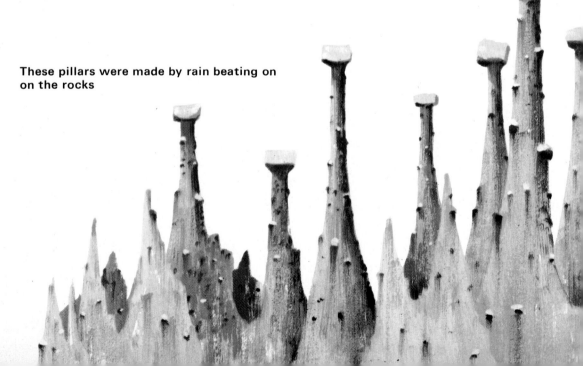

Scree

Frost and ice break
up the rock on
mountain slopes

Shattering the rocks

When the Sun shines on rocks, especially in the deserts, it can make them so hot that they expand. At night it gets cold and the rocks shrink again. This is a great strain on the rocks. They crack and split. Layers break off.

High in the mountains, and in the cold polar lands, the cold and ice break off pieces of rock. These pieces tumble down the slopes and pile up in great banks called scree.

Stone statues are worn away

Weather damage in cities

In the air over cities there are often a lot of gases and dust from factories. The rain falling through the air is turned into a weak acid. The acid eats into paint, stone and even steel. Buildings and statues are ruined.

The Work of the Wind

Hard rock

Soft rock

Wind, frost and rain attack the rocks

Rocks with odd shapes

Rocks may be worn into odd shapes by the weather. Sometimes they look like tall men standing in rows. Others look like mushrooms. Some rocks are made of hard and soft layers. The snow, ice, rain and wind wear away the soft rock more quickly. The hard parts are left behind.

Rocks shaped by the wind

When the weather has been very dry, the wind carries small pieces of dust and soil. In deserts, the wind lifts grains of sand and bounces them along. Armed with these sharp sand grains, the wind cuts into the rocks. The rocks are slowly worn into strange shapes or even into arches. The bits of rock that break off help to make new sand.

Seas of sand

As the wind blows across some deserts it leaves bare, wind-swept rocks. Other deserts look like seas of sand. The wind blows the sand into dunes. Some sand dunes are ridges hundreds of kilometres long. These are called seif dunes.

Other dunes are hills shaped like crescents, or quarter moons. These are called barchans. As the wind blows, these barchans move slowly forward. Sometimes they bury villages in their path.

Barchans are crescent shaped

Seif dunes are shaped like swords

Strange shapes are carved in the desert

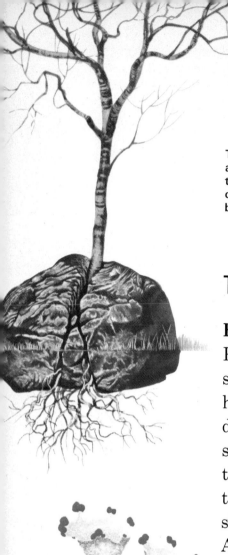

The roots of trees and plants force their way into cracks. The rocks break up

The Work of Plants and Animals

How plants break up rocks

Plants help to break up the rocks. Trees can split great boulders in two. Smaller plants also help to break up rocks. Their roots spread downwards and outwards. At first, the roots seem small and unimportant. Slowly they grow thicker and longer. They grow into cracks in the rocks and widen them. In this way whole slabs of rock are broken into many pieces.
As plants grow and as they die and decay they make acids that break up the rocks beneath the soil.

Lichen

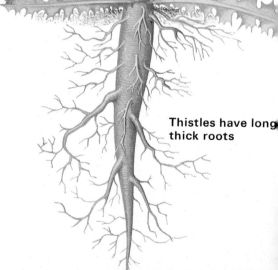

Lichens are plants that grow in patches on rocks. They are found high on mountains and in the cold lands when the winter snows have melted away. They produce acids. These acids slowly break up the rocks.

Thistles have long thick roots

Badgers dig burrows

The work of animals

Some animals, earthworms and insects help to break up rocks. Badgers and moles are two of these animals. When they dig burrows they throw out stones and small rocks with the soil. The weather attacks the stones and rocks and breaks them up.

Earthworms break up the soil as they tunnel underground. This makes the soil softer and helps the plants to get more air and water.

Ants make nests underground. They bring up soil and rocks as they build tunnels and rooms in the earth.

Termites, wasps, and burrowing spiders also dig holes in the ground. They help to break up rocks and change the soil.

Ant

Burrowing spider

Moles and earthworms make holes in the ground

How Soil is Made

Plants which grow in the soil help to protect it. The plant roots hold the soil together. When leaves decay they form a dark layer on top of the soil. This layer is called humus. It helps to keep the soil moist.

Some soils are good for plants

Crops are grown in places with good soil

Soil for farming

The soil provides plants with most of the food they need to grow. Good soil is fertile. It has taken thousands of years to form. When farmers plough the land and sow crops they must take care not to rob the soil of its goodness.

Types of soil

There are many different types of soil. Some soils are formed under heather and pine trees. These are not very fertile soils. Other soils form where there is moist grass and forests of broad-leaved trees. These are fertile soils. In the deserts plants do not grow for a long enough time for soil to form. They only appear after sudden rain storms.

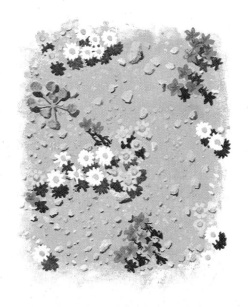

Deserts do not have good soil

Farmers cut down trees

Animals eat small trees and plants

Too many animals graze on dry land

The soil is soon washed away

How people change the soil

People have often been careless about the soil. They have cut
down trees for timber and cleared trees and bushes for farmland.
Some farmers have grazed too many animals in small areas.
When there are no trees and plants to hold the soil down, it is
easily carried away. It is washed away by the rain and blown
away by the wind. On slopes, the rain runs more quickly to the
rivers. Great floods are caused.

There are ways that people can protect the soil. Farmers can
plant rows of trees to stop the wind. In some desert areas,
cacti have been planted. Their roots spread out and hold the
sandy soil. Irrigation also helps. It keeps the soil moist so it
does not blow away.

The Work of Rivers

The course of a river

The water from rain and melting snow runs back from the land towards the sea. It usually flows in narrow channels as streams or as rivers. The path it takes is the course of the river.

Some rainwater dries up quickly in the hot sunshine. Some runs off the land straight into the streams and rivers. Some soaks down into the soil and into the rocks. It may come to the surface again in springs in other places.

The place where a river begins is called its source. This is usually an underground spring. At first the river is only a stream called a headstream. Most headstreams are high in the hills. All rivers follow a course that leads down towards the sea. The point at which a river enters the sea is called its mouth.

The course of a river

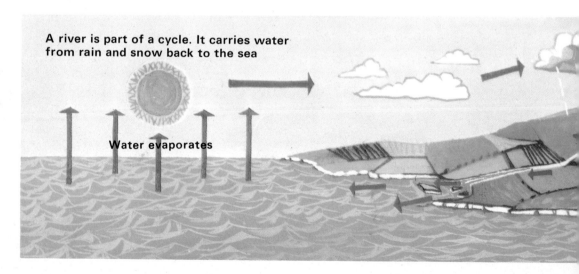

A river is part of a cycle. It carries water from rain and snow back to the sea

Water evaporates

In youth, a river runs quickly. It cuts a deep valley

A river near its source

Rivers carry away rocks and soil. In the hills the water runs quickly. It cascades down rapids and over waterfalls. The rocks and soil in the water swirl round and cut into the land. They slowly cut deep valleys. Even the waterfalls wear away.

Waterfalls usually fall over a layer of hard rock

Snow falls

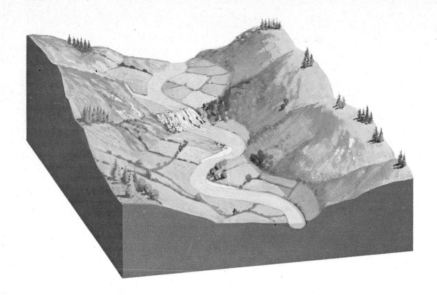

In middle age, a river cuts a wide valley as it winds about

River valleys

The valley that a river cuts is always changing shape. At first, the river cuts a deep valley with steep sides. Then the river begins to cut sideways as well. As it does so it makes the valley wider.

When you go round a bend in the road in a car you are thrown to one side. In the same way, water that goes round a bend in a river is thrown to the outside of the bend. The small bits of rock swirling round in the water cut into the banks. They form a cliff at the side of the valley.

Many plants grow along the water's edge

River gorges and canyons

Gorges and canyons are steep-sided valleys. They may be found anywhere along a river. The Grand Canyon in the United States is about two kilometres deep. It is being cut by the Colorado River. Gorges form where the rock is hard or where the sides of a valley do not wear down easily.

The Grand Canyon

River plains

Inside the bends of a river there is level ground. The water flows slowly here. The mud, sand and pebbles that were being carried along are dropped. A small plain is built up. When there has been a storm the river may flow over its banks and flood this plain. The mud and sand left behind by the river make good soil. Farmers may use the meadows on this plain to graze their cattle or to grow crops.

Beautiful plants like irises live in the water at the edge of slow rivers. The plants have tall, strong stems. The flowers are at the top of the stems so that the water will not crush them. Willow trees and many other plants grow well in the damp earth.

113

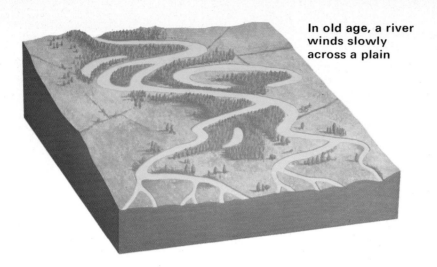

In old age, a river winds slowly across a plain

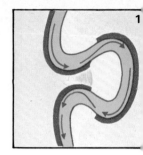

A meander

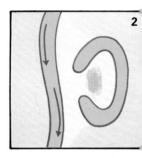

When a meander is cut off, it makes a lake

Many plants and animals live in the slow-moving part of a river

A river near the sea

A river often flows slowly across a broad plain before it reaches the sea. It now moves in giant loops called meanders. Here the river drops the stones and fine mud which it has been carrying. Hiding beneath the stones in the water there may be crayfish and freshwater shrimps. The plain is so flat that it is easily flooded. Then, fresh mud is dropped over it.

Crayfish

Freshwater shrimps

114

At Sydney Harbour several rivers flow into the sea

The river mouth

Some rivers have a very long journey to the sea. Others plunge straight down from the mountains. A few rivers end their journeys in lakes. The end of the river is called its mouth.

At its mouth, the river deposits the fine mud and stones it has been carrying. It may form new land called a delta. If the river has a wide mouth, or estuary, the mud may be dropped along the banks.

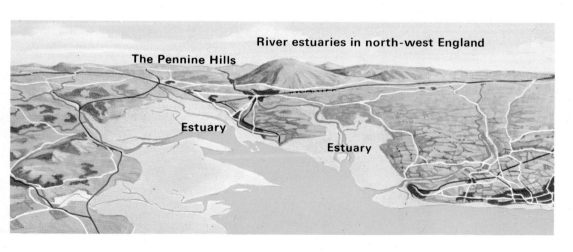

River estuaries in north-west England

The Pennine Hills

Estuary

Estuary

Underground Water

Water can be brought up from deep under
the ground

Springs and wells

When it rains most of the water sinks into the rocks. Even in
deserts water can be found deep down in the rocks. This water
may have fallen in places hundreds of kilometres away. It has
then passed along the layers of the rocks. Some of this
underground water comes back to the surface as springs. In wet
lands springs are the source of streams and rivers. In the deserts
the water bubbles up at oases.

In some parts of the world valuable stores of water lie deep
underground. The water is trapped between layers of waterproof
rocks. When wells are drilled through these rocks the water
gushes to the surface.

Underground water comes out from an
artesian well

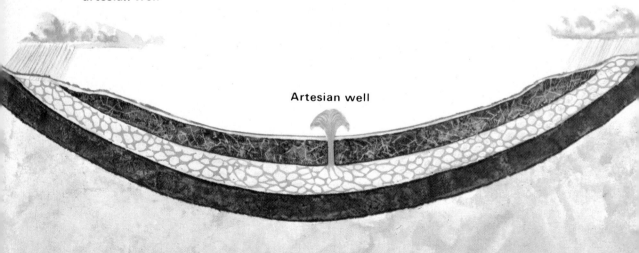

Artesian well

Vanishing rivers

Limestone is a rock that lets water pass through it. Rain quickly sinks into it. Streams and rivers that flow onto limestone from other rocks soon disappear underground. They flow along cracks in the limestone and make caves.

Cave bats

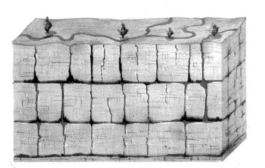
Water begins to wear the rocks away

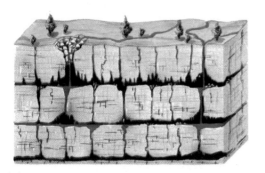
Slowly the holes become larger

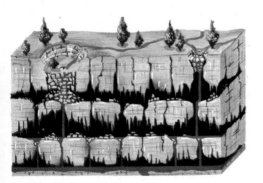
Finally, huge caves are formed

Underground caves

Bats led people to find the largest caves in the world. Millions of them were seen flying each night from their homes in the Carlsbad Caverns of New Mexico in the United States.

How caves form

Water forms a weak acid when it touches limestone. This acid attacks the mineral called calcium from which limestone is made. The water that flows underground makes wider and wider cracks in the limestone. In places it makes huge holes. Some holes become very big caves.

There are limestone caves in many countries. Thousands of people visit the Luray Caverns in the United States and the caves at Postojna in Yugoslavia.

Exploring underground caves

Streams make holes called swallow holes when they disappear into the limestone. Explorers often use these swallow holes to find underground caves. Exploring caves can be very dangerous. There are narrow passages to crawl through. There are steep drops, deep streams, and high waterfalls.

Exploring caves

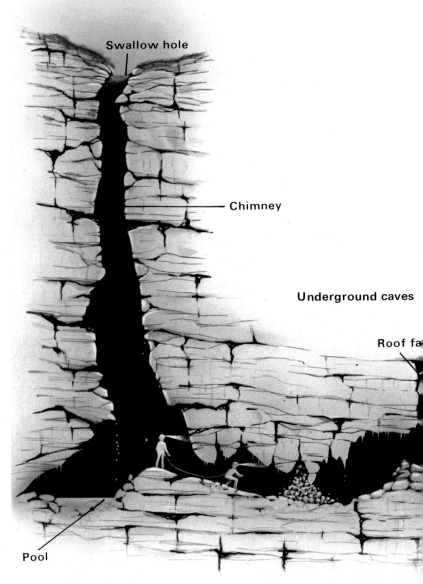

Swallow hole

Chimney

Underground caves

Roof fa

Pool

Wonders below the ground

In some parts of the world exploring caves is a popular sport. The explorers wear miners' helmets fitted with lamps so that they can see the wonderful sights in a cave.

Thousands of years ago people and animals may have used the cave for shelter. Cave explorers sometimes find their bones, tools and the remains of their meals near the entrance of the cave.

Stalagmites point upwards. Stalactites point downwards

As the explorers go further below ground, they pass along dark, damp passages. In the streams they may find pebbles covered in such pure white lime that they are called cave pearls. In the pools they may see fish without eyes darting through the water. They may suddenly find themselves in a huge cavern. Here beautiful rock shapes like icicles hang from the roof and grow up from the floor. These are called stalactites and stalagmites. Sometimes they join to form pillars. They are formed over hundreds of years. As the water drips through the cave, it leaves behind the lime that builds these strange sights.

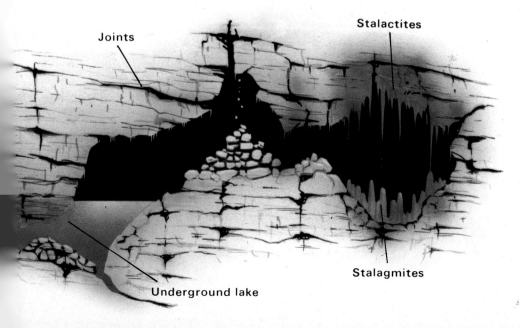

Joints

Stalactites

Underground lake

Stalagmites

Snow field

Glacier

The Work of Glaciers

The Gross Glockner glacier in Austria

About a million years ago the Great Ice Age began. Vast ice sheets built up and moved outwards across parts of the Earth. As the ice advanced, mammoths and other animals had to move. The ice sheets scraped the land clear of soil. They smoothed the valleys and the tops of hills. They carried the soil, stones and huge boulders for hundreds of kilometres. Then the ice began to melt. The rocks and boulders were dropped over the countryside. Today the ice is left in only a few areas. There are still thick ice sheets in Greenland and the Antarctic. There are smaller ones in Norway and Iceland. In the world's high mountains there are rivers of slowly moving ice called glaciers. Scientists study the ice to find out how long ago it was formed. They keep records so they will know how fast the ice is moving.

The Gross Glockner glacier is in Austria, high up in the Alps. The snow builds up in winter year after year. It becomes pressed into ice. The ice then slowly moves downhill as a glacier.

120

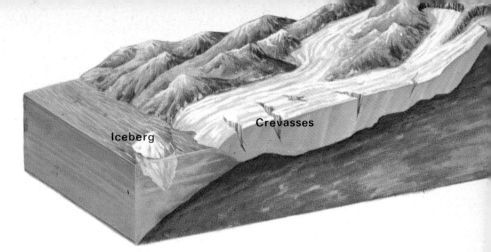

A glacier moves down to the sea

Iceberg

Crevasses

How the ice shapes the land

During the Great Ice Age the glaciers moved down valleys that were first made by rivers. They altered the shape of these valleys and made the sides smoother.

As a glacier moves, it splits into great cracks called crevasses. Stones and boulders fall into these crevasses from the sides of the valley. They become trapped in the ice. As the ice moves along it carries the stones and boulders with it. They scrape away the rocks beneath. The glacier is like a giant file. If the glacier reaches the sea before it melts, huge pieces break off. They fall into the sea. These giant pieces of ice are then known as icebergs. They can be very dangerous to ships.

Mammoths lived in the Ice Age

Ice and stones scrape away the sides and bottom of a valley

Moving glacier

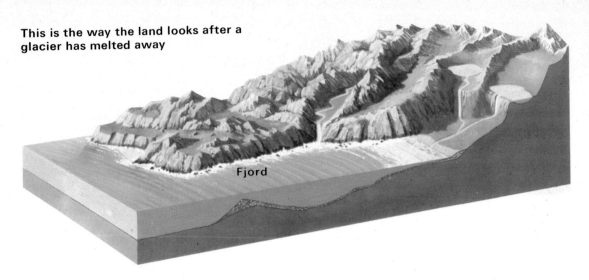

This is the way the land looks after a glacier has melted away

Fjord

Ice sheets drop large boulders when they melt. These are called erratics

The ice makes low hills called drumlins

Ice movement

After the ice has gone

In places where the ice has melted we can see how it has shaped the land. Valleys have been made smooth and deep. Waterfalls cascade from small valleys into deeper ones. Where the glacier began high in the mountains, great hollows have been scooped out by the ice. These hollows may now hold long, narrow lakes. Down by the coast the sea may have flooded the valley once filled by the glacier. There may now be a long, narrow inlet called a fjord. There are many fjords in Norway and New Zealand.

On the plains the ice sheets have left behind masses of clay. They have also dumped huge boulders. Sometimes the clay and stones have been shaped into low hills called drumlins.

122

A valley shaped by a glacier

Long ago there was a glacier in the valley shown on this page. Before the ice filled it, the valley was shaped like a letter V. Now it has been shaped like a letter U. When the ice melted it left behind rocks and clay on the valley floor. They have made large mounds called moraines. After the ice melted the weather became warmer. Plants grew and soil has formed. But the sides of the valley are still bare rock.

The Work of the Sea

The sea-shore is always changing. In some
places the sea builds it up. In others the sea
wears it away

The coast is the place where the land meets the sea. All the time its shape is being changed by the waves. The sea-shore lies along the coast. Sea-shores can be sandy, muddy or rocky. Some sea-shores have cliffs along them. Others have sand dunes behind them. The flattest part of the sea-shore is the beach. It slopes down gently, or sometimes steeply, towards the sea.

Groyne

A groyne traps sand and pebbles

The sand that you dig on the beach is made of very small pieces of rock. When the tide comes in, the waves carry the sand along the shore. They also carry large pebbles. In some places barriers called groynes have been built across the beach to stop the sand and pebbles from drifting away.

A sandy beach looks empty when the tide is out. But there are lots of animals in the sand, or left in the pools. Some animals, such as crabs, bury themselves. Others, such as starfishes and sea urchins, may have been washed up on the beach.

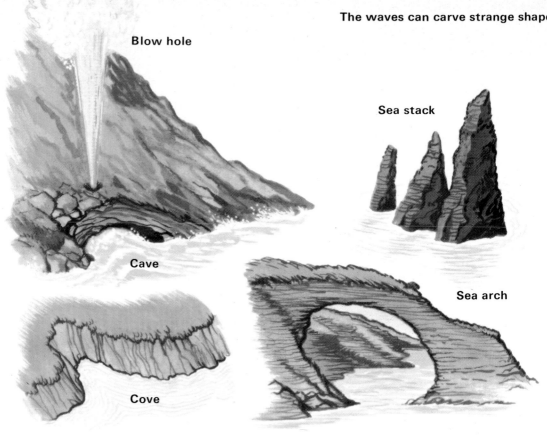

Blow hole

Sea stack

Cave

Sea arch

Cove

When the top of an arch caves in, sea pillars are left.

Rocks shaped by the sea

Sea cliffs along a rocky coast may have many strange shapes. All these shapes have been carved by the waves. Tall columns of rock may stand in the sea close by the cliffs. These are called sea stacks. Sometimes there is an arch right through the rocks. If you watch the waves beating against the cliffs you will see them lapping into small cracks and bays. Sometimes the water blows out above the cliffs from a hole at the back of a cave.

126

Danger along the cliffs

Sea waves often beat against the cliffs with terrific force. In a storm they can move rocks as large as a house. The waves throw sand and pebbles against the cliffs. Gradually the cliffs are undermined. The land slips and crashes to the beach below.

New land in the sea

Waves wear away the rocks that fall from the cliffs. They wear them down into smooth pebbles and grains of sand. If you look out across a bay you may see a ridge of sand and pebbles. It may stretch across the mouth of the bay as if to bar the waves from coming in. This is a bay bar. Here the sea is building new land. It is dropping the sand and pebbles that the waves are carrying along the shore. Sometimes sandy ridges link small islands to the coast.

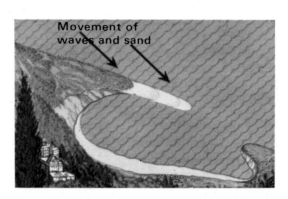

A bay bar

An island linked to the coast by sand

Waves undercut the cliffs. Huge rocks crash into the sea

Bulldozers dig up rocks under the soil

Sandstone

Granite

Quartz

Limestone

Conglomerate

ROCKS AND MINERALS

The Earth we live on is covered with rocks. In many parts of the world they are hidden beneath the grass and soil. But they can be seen in the deserts and the cliffs beside the sea.

Rocks are made of minerals. Some minerals, such as quartz, form beautiful crystals of many shapes and colours.

There are many different kinds of rocks. Some, like granite, are hard. Others, like sandstone, have small hard grains. Limestone comes from the remains of animals. Coal has formed from the remains of plants. Conglomerate is formed from bits of other rocks naturally cemented together.

People use rocks for buildings and to make all sorts of things in factories. They have cut mines and quarries into the Earth to get them out.

Rocks Made by Fire

Long ago the Earth was a huge ball of hot molten minerals. Slowly it began to cool. The outside grew hard and turned into rocks. They made a crust round the Earth. These rocks are called igneous rocks. Igneous means made by fire.

Deep down in the Earth it is still hot. Sometimes hot, molten rock called magma rises up towards the surface. Some of it cools down, deep inside the crust. It becomes a hard rock, granite.

Sometimes the molten liquid rock bursts out from volcanoes. It is then called lava. It cools down to form different rocks. One of these rocks is obsidian. It is hard, black and shiny. Another is pumice. This is the lightest rock known. It has so many air bubbles that it floats on water.

Pumice

Obsidian

Some igneous rocks cool inside the Earth. Others come from the lava of volcanoes.

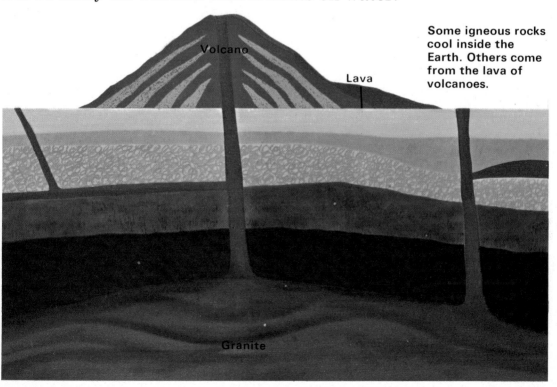

Volcano

Lava

Granite

Granite hills

The countryside around you has been carved from the rocks. In places, hills of granite may rise up above the surrounding land. This granite was once deep beneath the Earth. The rocks that were above it have gone. They have been broken up and carried away by the rain, the wind and ice. Hard granite wears away more slowly.

A granite hill

The columns of the Giant's Causeway

A strange lava flow

Some rocks in Northern Ireland are a strange shape. They are like columns piled alongside each other. People used to think that they were built by giants to get from Ireland to Scotland. They called them the Giant's Causeway. We now know that the rocks were once lava that poured from a crack in the Earth. It cooled quickly and formed these strange columns.

The Giant's Causeway

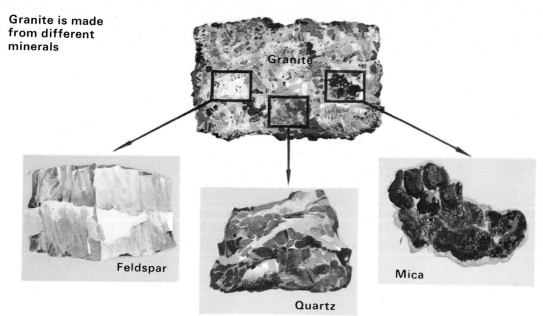

Granite is made from different minerals

Granite

Feldspar

Quartz

Mica

Building with granite

If you look at the polished stone on the front of a building, you may see it shine and sparkle. The colours you can see in the rock are the different minerals.

Granite has different colours in it. It has grey, pink, white and yellow. These are the colours of the different minerals. The minerals in granite are feldspar, quartz and mica.

Granite is a good building stone. It is strong and long-lasting. When it is polished it is beautiful. Builders sometimes use it to decorate important buildings. Large blocks are used for harbour walls. They can resist the strong waves.

Many buildings are made from granite

Conglomerate

Breccia

Rocks in Layers

Shake a mixture of sand, soil and pebbles in a glass jar that is half-filled with water. Let it stand for a few hours. You will see a layer of pebbles at the bottom and layers of sand and soil at the top. Bits that sink to the bottom of water like this are called sediments.

Some rocks are formed from sediments. The weather breaks the rock on the land into small pieces. Rivers, glaciers and the wind carry them into lakes and the seas. They sink to the bottom in layers. These layers are called strata Rocks made like this are sedimentary rocks.

Sedimentary rocks are made from bits of other rocks

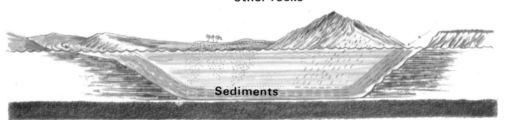

Sediments

Some sedimentary rocks

Conglomerate is a sedimentary rock. It is made from pebbles that have become cemented together. Breccia is made of quite large pieces of jagged rock. Shale and sandstone are made of very small pieces that are cemented together. Limestone was formed from the shells of dead sea animals. Coal was formed from plants.

Shale

An Indian temple made from sandstone

Sandstone

Using sandstone and limestone

People use sedimentary rocks for many things. Sandstone and limestone are useful rocks for building. They are easy to cut and shape. In the quarries special saws are used to mine them. Sandstone may be red, yellow, grey or white. Limestone is grey, white or yellow. In India, many temples are built from blocks of sandstone. Limestone is used in many countries for important public buildings.

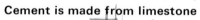
Cement is made from limestone

Sedimentary rocks are often ground up in factories. Farmers use ground limestone to improve the soil. It is also used in cement, toothpaste and paint. Sandstone is ground up to make glass.

Limestone

Seams of coal

Under the ground coal lies in layers called seams. Coal is made from forests that grew millions of years ago. These forests were buried by sand and clay when they were flooded by the sea. Over millions of years the sand and clay turned into sandstone and shale. The trees and plants turned into coal. Seams of coal are found between the layers of sandstone and shale.

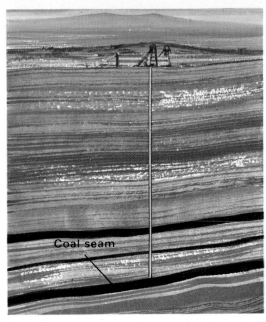

Coal seam

Many coal seams are deep underground

Coal is made from trees and plants that lived millions of years ago

Digging for coal

People have used coal for a long time. They burn it for fuel. They make gas and chemicals from it. Huge machines are used to dig up the coal near the surface. The seams deep down are dug by miners working in tunnels.

Coal

A plant fossil in coal

Oil in rocks

Oil is another fuel found in the Earth's rocks. It is probably made from tiny sea creatures that lived millions of years ago. When they died, they sank to the sea bed. They were buried by sand and mud. Over millions of years they turned into tiny drops of oil.

Oil is made from tiny sea creatures

How the oil became trapped

Long ago the thousands of tiny drops of oil that were in the spaces between the grains of sandstone and limestone rose upwards. In some places there was a layer of clay above. The oil could not get through the clay. It was trapped.

When men drill through the rocks, they find the oil. They also find natural gas and water trapped in the rocks.

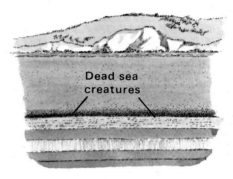

The sea creatures died and fell to the sea bed

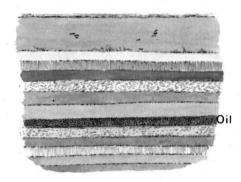

After many years, they became drops of oil in the sediments

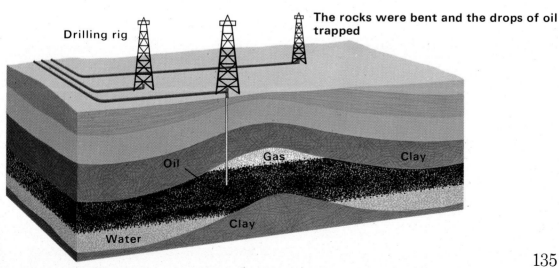

The rocks were bent and the drops of oil trapped

Drilling rig

Oil

Gas

Clay

Clay

Water

Changed Rocks

Some rocks were once other kinds of rocks. Quartzite, a very hard rock, was once sandstone. Gneiss (which sounds like 'nice'), is another very hard rock. Once it was granite. Gneiss has the same minerals as granite. But it does not look like granite. It has light and dark bands. These changed rocks are called metamorphic rocks.

These rocks were changed because of great forces in the Earth. When the Earth's crust moves, parts are pressed down inside. It is very hot deep inside the Earth and the heat melts the rocks. When they cool again they have changed. Sometimes the pressing itself is enough to change the rocks. Slate is another metamorphic rock. Once it was shale. Pressure changed the shale from a soft rock to hard slate.

Quartzite

Gneiss

Slate

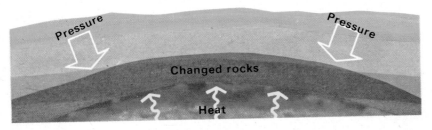

Metamorphic rocks were formed under great heat and pressure

136

Marble

Marble quarries

Marble is another metamorphic rock. Once it was limestone. Marble may be black, yellow, brown, green, pink or pure white. It feels cold when you touch it. Quarry saws can be used to cut marble. But in some quarries the marble is still cut carefully by hand.

Using marble

Many famous buildings are made of marble. Long ago the Greeks used marble to build the Parthenon in Athens. It has different colours at different times of day.

Sculptors use marble to make statues and monuments. The Greeks made many beautiful statues of their gods.

Marble is cut from quarries

The Parthenon in Athens, Greece, is built from marble

Chrysotile rock

Chrysotile fibres

Minerals and Metals

Rocks are made of different minerals. People use these minerals for many important things. Scientists examine rocks to see if they contain valuable minerals.

Some useful minerals

One useful mineral is chrysotile. If you looked at it carefully you would see that it was made of millions of small fibres. These fibres can be spun into thread and woven into cloth. The cloth from chrysotile and other minerals with fibres is called asbestos. Because asbestos is made of rock, it does not burn.

You may have seen firemen dressed in special white suits when they are fighting a fierce fire. These suits are made of asbestos. They protect the firemen from the flames.

Asbestos is also used for the lining of brakes in cars and for safety curtains in theatres.

Asbestos suits

Amethyst

Barytes

Pyrites

Smoky quartz

Blue calcite

Strontianite

Apatite

Jasper

Graphite

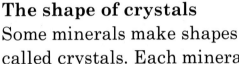
Citrine

The shape of crystals

Some minerals make shapes called crystals. Each mineral has its own crystal shape. People who study minerals are called mineralogists. By looking at the shape of a crystal they can tell the type of mineral.

There are many strange crystal shapes. Pyrites is made of iron. Some pyrites crystals are shaped like a cube. Table salt is also made of small cubes. Some calcite crystals are shaped like pyramids. They look like dogs' teeth, Strontianite has pencil-shaped crystals with six sides. Wulfenite has bright red crystals. They are flat and look like small table tops.

Dolomite

Wulfenite

Tourmaline

Native copper

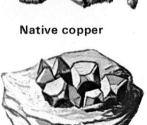
Crystals of copper pyrites

What are metals?

Some minerals are called metals. Most metals are found in the ground in mixtures called ores. Copper is an important metal. One copper ore is called peacock ore. It has all the colours of a peacock's tail. Some copper is found as solid lumps of metal. When metals are found like this they are known as native metals.

A brass trumpet

Zinc

THE ORES OF IRON

Things made of metal

People have found many uses for metals. Metals can be mixed together to make an alloy. Copper and zinc are mixed to make an alloy called brass. A trumpet is made from brass.

Iron comes from several different ores. It is made into steel. A bicycle is made mainly of iron and steel. To stop steel rusting, it can be coated with chrome or tin.

Haematite

Limo

Iron pyrites

A bicycle is made of iron, steel, and tin

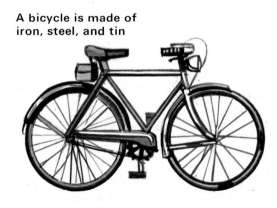

Cassiterite, the ore of tin

Magnetite

Looking for gold

Precious metals

Gold, silver and platinum are valuable. Because
they are hard to find, they are called precious
metals. Some things are made of solid gold and
silver. Others are made of different metals and
covered with a thin layer of silver or gold.
Forks, pens and cups may be made of solid gold
or silver. Or they may just have gold or silver
on top.

Some gold is found at the bottom of streams.
Many people used to hunt for gold. They
washed stones and mud in a pan. They looked
carefully to find shining pieces of gold.
Sometimes they found only shining crystals of
iron pyrites. This looked like gold but it was
not valuable. The gold hunters called iron
pyrites 'Fool's Gold'. Today most gold comes
from South Africa.

Platinum is more valuable than either gold
or silver. Small grains of platinum are found
inside rocks. It is expensive to get them out.
Platinum is used to make jewellery. Some tools
needed by scientists are also made of platinum.

Gold

Silver

Platinum

141

Precious Stones

Some mineral crystals are hard to find. These are called precious stones. They are very valuable. The most precious stones are diamonds, emeralds, rubies and sapphires.

Precious stones are cut and polished to make beautiful gems. They are worn in rings and in other jewellery.

Diamond

Emerald

Ruby

Sapphire

BIRTHSTONES

JANUARY
Garnet

JULY
Ruby

FEBRUARY
Amethyst

AUGUST
Sardonyx

MARCH
Bloodstone

SEPTEMBER
Sapphire

APRIL
Diamond

OCTOBER
Opal

MAY
Emerald

NOVEMBER
Topaz

JUNE
Pearl

DECEMBER
Turquoise

Semi-precious stones

Other gems can be found more easily. These are semi-precious stones. They are also cut and polished to make jewellery.

In the past, people used to think gems had magical power. Amethysts are one of the most beautiful stones. At one time people thought the amethyst was a love charm. They also thought it helped people to sleep and kept away thieves.

Some stones are said to bring special luck to people born in different months of the year. These are called birthstones. Do you know what your birthstone is?

The Canning Jewel

Making jewellery

Gems look beautiful when they are cut. The people of ancient Babylon were the first to cut stones. They shaped them into smooth ovals. Then they cut them so that they shone and sparkled. Some pieces of jewellery are very famous. They are kept in museums. One famous jewel is made like a merman. His body is made from a large pearl. This jewel also has diamonds and rubies.

SEMI-PRECIOUS STONES

Pyrope

Topaz

Zircon

Spinel

Amethyst

Almandite

Tourmaline

Black opal

Spessartite

Yellow beryl

Green beryl

Demantoid

Green tourmaline

Moonstone

Hessonite

Jasper

Turquoise

Aquamarine

THE EARTH'S STORY

How the Earth began

Nobody knows exactly how the Earth was formed. Not long ago scientists thought it came from the Sun. They thought that a star passed so close to the Sun that it pulled great jets of gas from it. These gases then cooled down and formed the Earth and the other planets.

Today scientists believe that the Earth began in a cloud of dust. This cloud was swirling round in a spiral. Most of the dust became the Sun. The rest became the planets.

Some scientists think the Earth and other planets were formed when a star near our Sun exploded

The dust became so hot as it rushed together that it melted. Balls of liquid minerals were formed. One of these balls was the Earth. It started to cool and to become solid.

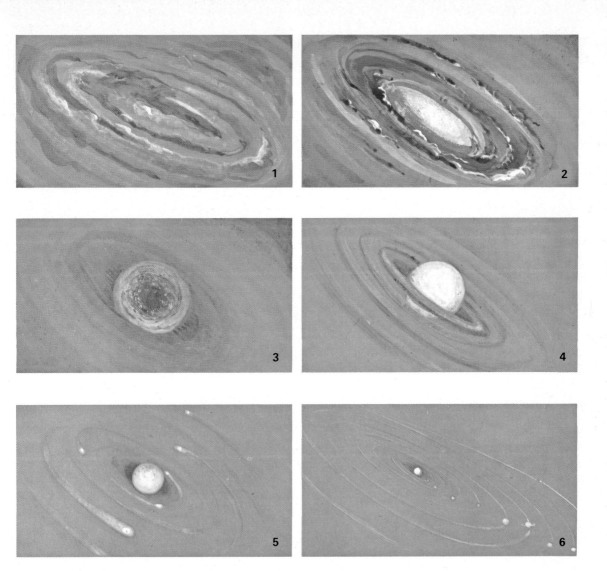

The Sun and planets may have begun as a cloud of dust

The first rocks, air and life

The light minerals in the liquid ball of the Earth rose to the surface. They cooled to form a crust of rocks.

At first, there was only bare rock. The hot minerals in the rocks gave off gases that formed the atmosphere. When these gases cooled, water was formed. It fell to the ground in great rainstorms and made the oceans. Then, millions of years later, the first simple form of life appeared in the oceans.

At first there was no life. Then the first cells appeared

How the Earth Tells its Story

If you put your hand in wet
cement it leaves behind a print.
In the same way raindrops
that fell millions of years ago
have left their prints. These
prints and the remains of the
plants and animals which lived
long ago are found in the rocks.
They are called fossils.

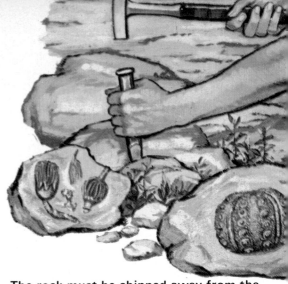

The rock must be chipped away from the fossil

How fossils are formed

Most fossils are formed when an animal or plant
falls into soft mud or sand and is quickly
buried. When the skeleton decays, it crumbles
away. It leaves behind a print in the rock
showing how it was shaped. This is called a
mould. Sometimes the mould is filled by more
mud and sand or by minerals. The filling
becomes solid and forms a cast. This cast looks
just like the skeleton.

Fossil rain spots

A trilobite

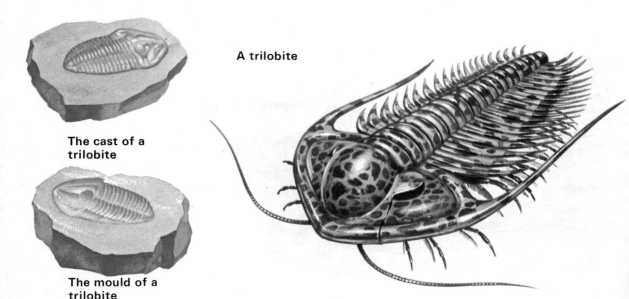

The cast of a
trilobite

The mould of a
trilobite

Fossils and evolution

Just over a hundred years ago people did not understand what fossils showed. They thought there had always been men, cats, sheep and trees on the Earth. In 1859, the scientist Charles Darwin startled people with his new ideas. He said

Charles Darwin

that animals and plants gradually changed over a long time. Only those best fitted to their surroundings could survive. If the only food was leaves in high trees then only the giraffes born with the longest necks would be able to live. In this way, he said, new types of plants and animals had slowly appeared. This change is called evolution. Fossils have shown how it has taken place. Horses, for example, have only one toe. Fossils show that millions of years ago they had four toes on their front feet and three toes on their back feet. These early horses were the size of a large dog.

The evolution of the horse

Eohippus   Mesohippus   Merychippus

Pliohippus   Modern horse

Fossil bones are carefully removed from the rock

The skeleton of
Iguanodon

Piecing fossils together

Fossils are usually found in rock. Geologists are the scientists
who study rocks. They look for fossils in bare rocks, such as sea
cliffs and quarries. They also examine rocks that have been
found by drilling deep into the Earth. Rocks called shales,
limestones, coal and sandstones are the main types of rocks that
contain fossils. Geologists do not look for fossils in rocks that
were once molten lava. Any animals or plants falling into the
lava would have been burned up.

A dinosaur skeleton
is put together in
a museum

Sometimes a geologist finds
the fossil remains of large
animals that lived millions of
years ago. He gently chips the
rock away. The fossil is made
of stone, but he must take great
care not to damage it. He takes
photographs to show how the
pieces look before they are
removed. Then he puts the
parts together again to show
the whole skeleton. Other
experts can then make a model.

148

Two fossil stories

From the study of fossils we know that the first animals with backbones to live on the land were amphibians. They evolved, or slowly changed, from animals that lived in the sea. Although amphibians lived on land, they laid their eggs in the sea. The fossil skeleton of Eryops shows it was as long as a crocodile.

At one time the only clue to the beginning of the birds was a single fossil feather. Now more fossils of a flying animal called Archaeopteryx have been found. A picture of the animal has been built up. But scientists still cannot agree if it was a flying reptile or the first bird. Archaeopteryx lived when dinosaurs ruled the land. It had teeth in its beak like the flying reptiles which lived at that time. But it had feathers on its wings like the birds living today.

Archaeopteryx

A fossil of Archaeopteryx

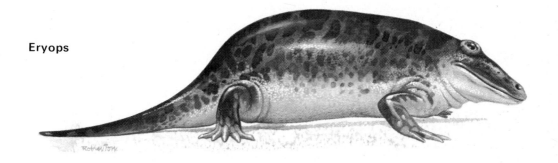

Eryops

A fossil of Eryops

149

Dating the Past

All living things contain carbon. When they die the carbon remains. After a long time this carbon changes into another type of carbon. It takes 70 thousand years to change. If the carbon in a fossil is only half changed it must be about 35 thousand years old. From carbon dating scientists can discover the age of any fossil with carbon.

Horsetails grew during the Carboniferous period. The fossil stem and leaves show how they looked

Forests of long ago
The time when coal was formed is called the Carboniferous period. There were great forests of ferns and plants. The carbon from these forests has shown they lived 300 million years ago.

Fern fossil   Tree bark fossil

Giant dragonflies lived 300 million years ago

A dragonfly fossil
The dragonfly was one of the first insects with wings. Fossils of dragonflies are found in Carboniferous rocks. They lived in the warm, damp forests. Some were very large. One fossil dragonfly found in France was a metre from wing tip to wing tip. When it died it left carbon remains. That helped scientists to find out how long ago it lived.

Pollen from ancient plants

Grains of pollen that dropped from flowers thousands of years ago can tell scientists what the climate was like then.
In some places, plants that lived in swamps did not rot away when they died. They built up layer on layer to form peat. There may be a layer with oak pollen at the bottom and a layer with pine pollen on top. This tells us that oak trees died out and pine forests then grew. The climate had become colder.

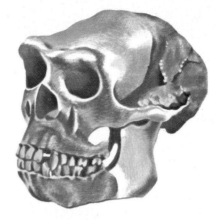

Fossil skull

Early tools

The first men

Fossil skulls of man's ancestors on Earth have been found in Java, Europe and China. But the oldest were found in Africa. They are over two million years old. Sometimes weapons and tools have been found in the same place. Pollen grains and carbon remains have helped to date these finds.

The scientists are taking a sample of peat to study the pollen layers

Pollen grains in peat show how plants in an area have changed. This shows how the climate has changed

Birch

Ash

Pine

Oak

The Ages of the Earth

Early horse

Rocky Mountains and Andes

400 m years

End of dinosaurs

First land plants

Sea lilies

4500 r years

Fishes

Birds

Flowering plants

100 million years ago

Trilobites

Pterodactyls

Mammals

Age of dinosaurs

200 mi years a

How old is the Earth?

People used to think that the Earth began only a few thousand years ago. They worked out that it began in exactly 4004BC. Now we know that it is so old that it is difficult to imagine a time so long ago.

Scientists say that the Earth is at least 4,500 million years old. They have searched and studied the rocks for clues to its age. They have dated fossils and measured natural radioactivity in the rocks. They have also measured the amount of salt that has gathered in the seas.

The spiral shows five thousand million years of the Earth's history. It shows the plants and animals that lived at various times

iant mmals

40 million years ago

Apes

Alps and Himalayas

Rapid spread of grasses

Age of amphibians

Ice Age

First life

Insects

Seaweeds

Protozoa and sponges

Giant ferns

Mammoth

Reptiles

Woolly rhinoceros

lachian s

Man

1 million years ago

Periods in the Earth's history

The clues from the rocks have shown how the rocks were formed. They have also shown what the world was like millions of years ago. Scientists have divided the history of the Earth into stretches of time called ages. There were ages when the only living things were in the sea, when dinosaurs ruled the Earth, and when there were great forests, deserts and ice sheets.

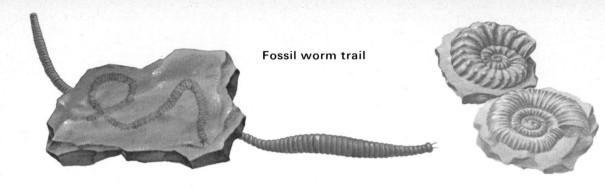

Fossil worm trail

Fossil ammonites

Life Begins in the Sea

Fossils of plants and animals in the rocks are the main clues that help us to piece together the story of the Earth. The earliest rocks do not show much sign of life. But that does not mean there was no life. The early rocks are so old and twisted that most fossils have been destroyed. But some worm trails and the remains of sponges have been found.

About 700 million years ago the shallow seas around the Earth teemed with life. This was the Cambrian period. It lasted for about 100 million years. There were sponges, jellyfish, sea-lilies, starfish, brachiopods, ammonites and trilobites. Some kinds of trilobites floated. Others were blind and crawled on the sea bed. They dug in the mud for their food.

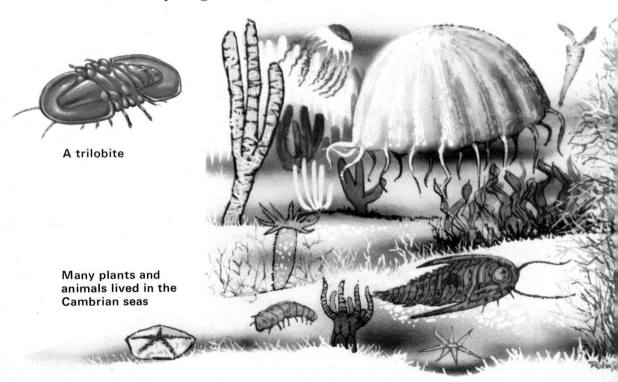

A trilobite

Many plants and animals lived in the Cambrian seas

Brachiopods lived in the sea for over 200 million years

The first fish did not have jaw bones

Placoderms were among the first fish with jaws

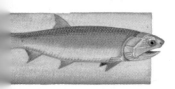

Paleoniscus was one of the first fish to have bones like those of most modern fish

The first Coelacanth lived millions of years ago. A few are still found today

New types of life

In the Ordovician and Silurian periods the climate was warm and pleasant. There were deserts in some places. But life remained in the seas. Some living things were like those that lived in the Cambrian seas. But by now there were many new creatures. Sea urchins and corals appeared. Great colonies of small animals called graptolites hung from seaweed that floated across the seas.

The age of fishes

The first fishes appeared at this time. They had no jaws and dug into the mud for their food. They were the first animals with backbones. Later fish had jaws, bones and air bladders. Some were 30 feet long. The Age of Fishes began when fishes took over the seas in the Devonian period. One type of fish from this period is still alive today. It is the Coelacanth.

The Silurian sea

The Age of Coal Forests

Coal is one of the rocks of the Carboniferous period. It is made from dead plants and so contains a lot of carbon. That is why this time is called the Carboniferous period.

Life in the sea was much the same as before. There were brachiopods, sea-lilies and some trilobites.

The land was covered in tall forests. The plants and trees were not like those of today. There were giant ferns, horsetails and scale trees. Huge insects and large amphibians lived in them.

A Carboniferous forest

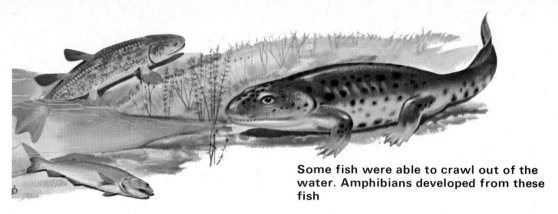

Some fish were able to crawl out of the water. Amphibians developed from these fish

How coal was formed

The warm wet forests lasted for a very long time. Coal is the remains of these dense forests. When the giant ferns and horsetails died they fell into swamps. Before they rotted they were covered in sand and mud. New forests grew on the sand and the mud. Then they too died and were covered in sand and mud. So layer on layer built up. The layers of sand and mud pressed down. Under the weight, the plants became peat and then coal.

A frog is a modern amphibian

The Age of Amphibians

As time passed, the world changed. In some parts the climate became dry. The rivers and ponds, where many fishes lived, dried up. Some fish could breathe out of water with the air bladder that helped them to float. They also had strong fins to push themselves across mud and on to the land.

As time went by some of these animals changed. They grew four legs and a long tail. These helped them to survive on the land. They were now amphibians. Amphibians live on the land most of the time. They go back to the water to lay their eggs. The Carboniferous period is called the Age of Amphibians.

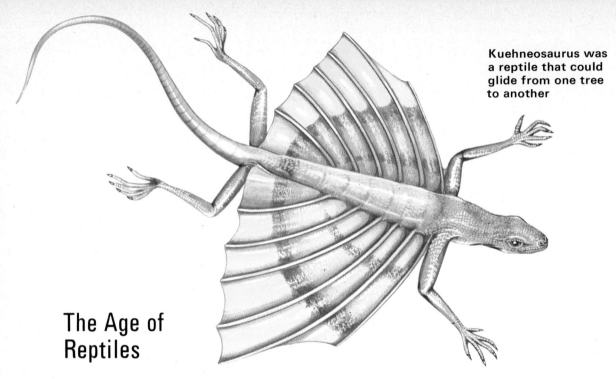

Kuehneosaurus was a reptile that could glide from one tree to another

The Age of Reptiles

After the Age of Amphibians the climate became drier and more suited to reptiles. Giant reptiles swooped across the sky. Others swam in the oceans. Monster reptiles lived on the land. Amphibians had to go back to the water to lay their eggs. But reptiles laid a different type of egg. Their young grew inside the egg. When they were hatched they could survive on the land. Reptiles had scales that stopped their skin drying out. Their legs stuck out beneath them so they could walk more easily on the land.

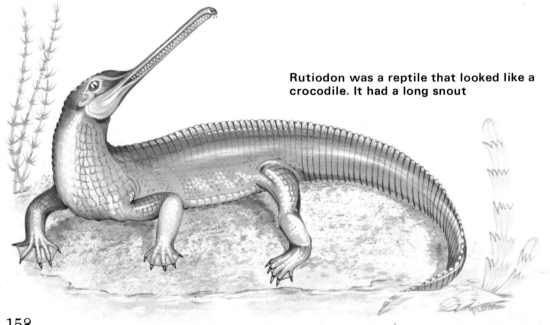

Rutiodon was a reptile that looked like a crocodile. It had a long snout

Dimetrodon was a meat-eating reptile

A strange reptile

Some reptiles looked very strange. One was called Dimetrodon. On its back was a big fin that looked like a sail. This fin helped to catch the heat from the Sun. Dimetrodon was a meat eater. It chased and ate smaller reptiles.

The first bird

Flying reptiles could escape from their enemies, such as Dimetrodon. But they could not fly properly. At last, they died out and birds with feathers took their place in the skies. Archaeopteryx was part reptile and part bird. It had the skull, teeth and tail of a reptile. But its feet and feathers were like a bird's.

Archaeopteryx

Tyrannosaurus

Brontosaurus

Triceratops

There were many different types of dinosaurs

Fossil dinosaur eggs have been found. They are much bigger than hens' eggs

Dinosaurs Rule the Land

Dinosaurs were reptiles that ruled the Earth for a hundred million years. Some were huge, fierce creatures. Others were small and harmless. They all laid eggs. The terrible Tyrannosaurus was the biggest meat eater. It was 6 metres tall and 13 metres long from head to tail. It had huge jaws and long, jagged teeth. Some dinosaurs could run fast enough to escape from Tyrannosaurus. Others had bony armour which helped to protect them. Triceratops had long sharp horns with which to fight back.

Diplodocus ate plants

Styracosaurus was five metres long

Many dinosaurs ate only plants. Long necks were a big advantage to these dinosaurs. They also had long tails to balance their long necks. Dinosaurs such as Brontosaurus could wade into the water to escape their meat-eating enemies. The water also supported them.

Reptiles that flew and swam

Not all reptiles lived on the land. Pteranodon was the largest flying reptile. When there was a wind it could glide over the sea for days looking for food. In the seas there were other great reptiles. Some had necks as long as their bodies. Their long necks made it easy for them to catch fish.

Pteranodon swoops down over the sea

The Age of Mammals began as dinosaurs died out

Mammals Take Over

Macrauchenia

Macrauchenia and Toxodon were early mammals

Toxodon

Nobody knows why the dinosaurs died out. Some people say that changes in the Earth's climate killed them. Others think that the first mammals ate their eggs. When the dinosaurs ruled the world, the first mammals were small rat-like animals. These mammals were covered in fur, unlike the scaly dinosaurs. The young of most mammals were born alive, not hatched from eggs. When the dinosaurs died out, the mammals could then thrive. Some ate plants and some ate insects. Others, like the fierce sabre-toothed tiger, ate other mammals.

A sabre-toothed tiger

A woolly mammoth

How mammals survived

The Age of Mammals began about 60 million years ago. The climate was warm and the mammals grew very large. There were pigs as big as donkeys. The ancestor of the horse ran across the grasslands. Giant birds lived in the trees of the forests. The first whales were living in the oceans.

Mammals could survive better than reptiles. They had better limbs. They could smell and hear better. Their brains were bigger. When the climate began to change they were more able to survive.

About a million years ago, the climate began to get very cold. Deep snow fell in the mountains. Sheets of ice began to cover the mountains and the land. The Great Ice Age had begun. Plants and animals died or retreated to the warmer lands. The animals that had changed could bear the cold. The woolly rhinoceros and the woolly mammoth had thick coats of fur that kept them warm.

Man Arrives on the Earth

Stone choppers were some of the first tools

Nobody is sure when people first appeared on the Earth. Our ancestors were living at the same time as the mammoths during the Ice Age. But the earliest remains have been found in the warmer lands of Africa. Here scientists have found fossils of skulls. One is nearly three million years old. It may be that of an early man.

The ancestors of people may have been ape-like mammals living in trees. When the forests began to disappear they came down from the trees. As time went by their feet, legs and backbones changed. They could then walk upright on two legs. Their arms and hands were left free to gather berries and other food.

The earliest people had brains that made them different from other animals. They learned to make simple tools with their hands. One of the first tools was a stone sharpened for hunting animals.

The ancestors of people ate wild fruit. They made tools to hunt animals

Tools for hunting

The tools that the earliest
people made helped them to
survive. They could defend
themselves against attack by
animals. They could hunt more
food with spears that they had
learned to make. The first
people also began to make tools
from bones as well as from
stone.

The ancestors of
people used
simple weapons
to fight wild
animals

Fire is discovered

Early people must have seen
fires caused by lightning and
by hot lava from volcanoes.
They may have discovered
how to make fire themselves
by twisting a stick very fast
against another piece of wood.
They could then cook food and
keep themselves warm.

Making fire was a big step forward

Arrowheads

Harpoons

Carefully made tools like these were used 30 thousand years ago

Early fishermen

Men who lived in the Stone Age, 30 thousand years ago, knew how to make fine tools from bone and stone. They made spearheads and arrowheads. They also invented the bow and arrow, a big step forward. Now men were able to hunt and kill animals that ran very fast. They also made bone harpoons for catching fish.

Early fishermen had to stand in the water, because they had no boats. They could catch only fish near the lake shores and river banks. Their first boats were probably tree trunks. Men then learned how to scrape out the inside of a tree trunk. They could then sit in it. They could fish away from the shores and banks. The first known boat was found in Holland. It was made eight thousand years ago. When men had boats they could begin to visit new places that they could not reach on foot.

People learned to make boats

Cave artists

Early people used their brains and hands to draw, paint and carve, as well as to hunt. Many of the caves where they lived have pictures of animals on the walls. They may have thought that drawing pictures of animals would mean there would always be plenty to hunt. They may have thought it would make them better hunters.

The early artists used the local earth for colours. They mixed it with fat to make the paint stick. They made paint brushes from leaves, animal fur or chewed twigs. Sometimes they blew paint round their hands to leave an outline.

Animals were painted on cave walls

Famous cave paintings

There are some famous cave paintings in Europe. Most of them are of animals. One shows a man dressed in animal skins. It was painted about 15 thousand years ago. The most famous cave paintings are in Altamira in Spain and in Lascaux in France.

People have learned to use the power of the water and wind

A silkworm

Clothing is made from a silkworm's cocoon

People have learned to farm the land

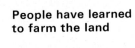

PEOPLE AND THE EARTH

Think of ten ways that people use the Earth. Now think of twenty. If you took the time you could probably think of a hundred. Our houses, food and clothes all come from the Earth and its plants and animals. People have invented a lot of new things. But even these come from what the Earth provides.

People have found ways to make the Earth work for them. They have made water-wheels to use the power of running rivers. They have also built windmills to use the wind.

Sometimes people have made very surprising discoveries. Long ago the Japanese learned how to make silk from a silkworm's cocoon. They made kimonos from the silk.

The soil is one of the Earth's greatest treasures. It is used to grow food for the millions of people on Earth.

Beautiful buildings have been made from stone and wood

People have used their hands and brains to turn stone and wood into beautiful buildings and places of worship. Many skilled craftsmen worked years to make them. There are beautiful cathedrals, temples, mosques and palaces in many lands.

Farming and Fishing

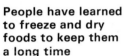
People have learned to freeze and dry foods to keep them a long time

A modern way to milk cows

Fresh peas   Dried peas

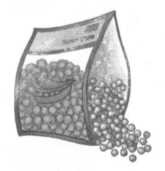
Frozen peas

An age-old way of growing rice

Our food comes from the Earth's plants and animals. Where the soil and climate are good, people can grow vast fields of wheat and corn. In some places, farmers have to irrigate the land because it is too dry. In others they add fertilizers to the soil to make it richer.

The number of people in the world grows every year. So more food is needed. Some machines have been made to help farmers. Milking machines help farmers to milk many cows at a time. Tractors plough fields quickly.

Modern machines are not used in all parts of the world. In some places, most farming is still done by hand. For some crops, this is better.

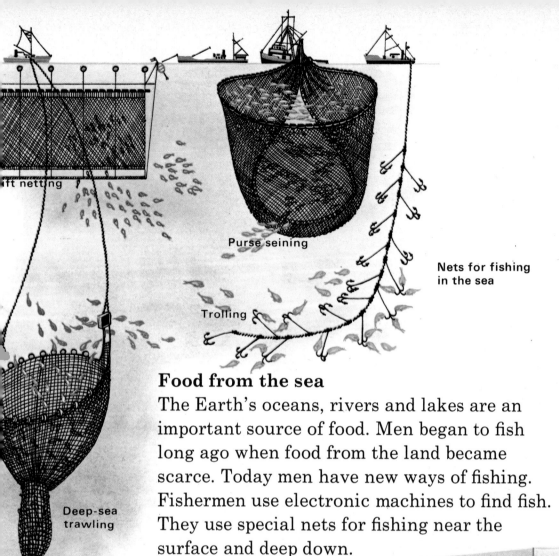

ft netting

Purse seining

Trolling

Nets for fishing
in the sea

Deep-sea
trawling

Food from the sea

The Earth's oceans, rivers and lakes are an
important source of food. Men began to fish
long ago when food from the land became
scarce. Today men have new ways of fishing.
Fishermen use electronic machines to find fish.
They use special nets for fishing near the
surface and deep down.

Fish farms

To get more food, fish farms
are being started. There are
fish farms in Japan. Here, fish
are hatched from eggs. They
are fed special food so that
they grow quickly. When they
grow bigger they are put in
tanks of seawater. Some fish
are eaten fresh from the tanks.
Others are frozen so they can
be kept for a long time.

Fish farming

Building Homes

People have always made their
homes from the things around
them. The first homes were
caves. Later people learned to
build shelters from branches.
They covered them with mud
and leaves. In some parts of
the world, they built huts of
stone. In others, long grasses
and animal skins were used.

A simple hut of woven branches

Homes in hot countries

People all over the world still build different kinds of houses.
That is because the weather is different. It is also because they
have to use different things for buildings.

In hot dry countries, houses are built to keep out the heat.
The walls are thick and are made of sun-baked mud. The windows
are small. They let in the light and the breezes.

Houses made of bricks

A Swiss chalet made of wood and stone

Homes in cold countries

In cold countries, houses are built to keep people warm. The roofs of many buildings in Switzerland are wide and sloping. Snow settles on the roof and helps to keep the house warm. There are many trees in Switzerland. The people have used the wood to build their homes. They have also used stone from the mountains.

Skyscrapers

Today people have found new ways of building. They use different materials. Tall skyscrapers made of iron, concrete and glass rise hundreds of metres into the air. Modern buildings of steel and concrete are found all over the world. They rise alongside the wooden buildings of Switzerland and next to the mud-brick homes in many desert towns.

Building a modern skyscraper of steel and cement

Towns and Cities

In some parts of the world most people live in a town or a city. Some of these are beautiful places. Others are ugly and dirty.

Some cities have big problems. People are crowded together in slums. The streets are packed with cars. Often there is noise and unclean air. Most of the plants and animals are gone. Tall buildings and concrete streets have taken their place.

Can the Earth support us?
The number of people in the world grows by over a million people every year. The Earth has to provide more food, clothes and buildings for them. Scientists say the Earth cannot provide enough for everyone. They point to all the rubbish that people waste. In the cities it is a problem to know what to do with it. Some scientists say we must find ways of using it to make new things.

A city's rubbish can be used to make new things

Pigeons live among the tall buildings of a modern city ▶

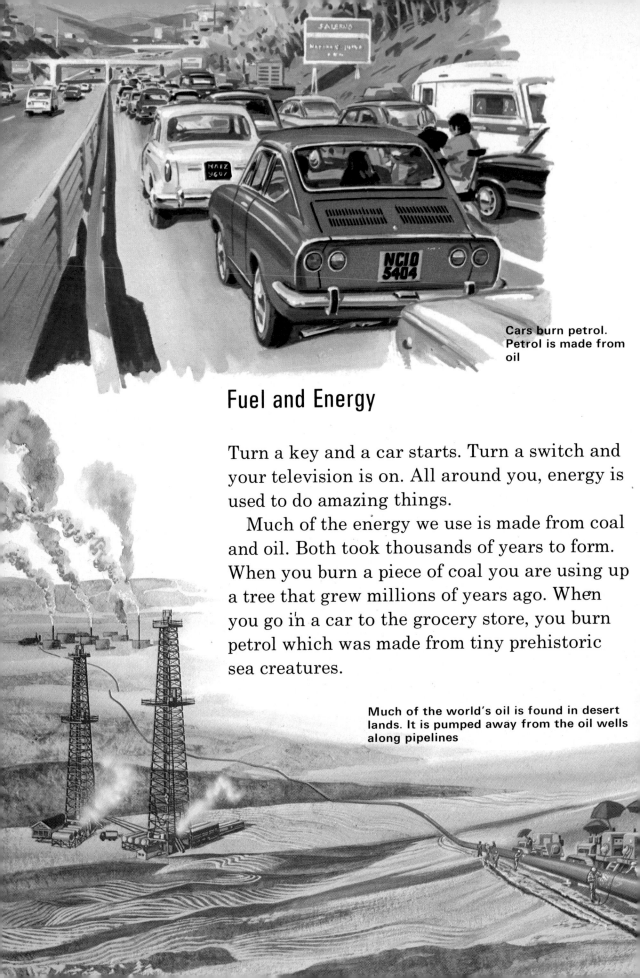

Cars burn petrol.
Petrol is made from
oil

Fuel and Energy

Turn a key and a car starts. Turn a switch and your television is on. All around you, energy is used to do amazing things.

Much of the energy we use is made from coal and oil. Both took thousands of years to form. When you burn a piece of coal you are using up a tree that grew millions of years ago. When you go in a car to the grocery store, you burn petrol which was made from tiny prehistoric sea creatures.

Much of the world's oil is found in desert lands. It is pumped away from the oil wells along pipelines

An electric record player

An electric typewriter

Making energy

We know that the coal and oil in the Earth cannot last forever. So other ways of making energy are being found.

Energy is made in power stations at dams. It is also made in nuclear power plants. But nuclear power plants make dangerous wastes. Scientists are looking for better ways to make energy without causing pollution. We may get energy from the Sun's heat in the future.

Electricity

Much of our energy is used to make electricity. Without it irons would not iron. Record players would not play. What else would not be possible?

An electric train signal

A power station

Lake

Dam

Power station

177

Printing cloth

Factories and Industries

Most of the things we use for everyday life come from the Earth. But we do not make them ourselves. They are made in factories.

The parts from which our houses are built have been made in factories. The clothes we wear were made in factories. The food we eat has often been tinned in factories. The cars and trains in which we ride were made in factories.

All kinds of fuels are used in factories. Coal, gas, oil and electricity are used for heating. Electricity powers lights and most machines.

Canning food

Machines

Men have invented many different machines. Some are large and heavy. In a cotton factory the cloth passes through heavy rollers and the pattern is printed on it. In a canning factory machines fill and label the cans.

Modern industry depends on metals. Steel is made in factories. It may then be moulded and welded to make more machines.

Welding iron

Pollution from factories

Only two hundred years have passed since men first used coal to drive their machines. This was called the Industrial Revolution. It began in Europe. It changed people's lives. It brought many good things. But it also caused some problems.

Cities and factories spread across the countryside. The factories dumped chemicals into rivers. The fuels burned in houses and factories made smoke. A chemical called sulphur in the fuels made a poisonous gas. It harmed people and plants.

In some places laws have been passed to stop pollution. The air and water have been made clean again.

Vanishing Animals

People have made many
changes in the Earth.
Sometimes these changes have
harmed wild animals.

Danger from farmers

Farmers clear away woods and
hedges to plough new land. The
animals lose their shelter and
food. Only the animals that can
feed on farmers' crops can
survive. Farmers think they are
pests and kill them.

When lands are cleared, animals lose their homes

Farmers add fertilizers to the soil to make
more plants grow. They spray plants to kill
insects. Animals get these chemicals in their
bodies. Many have died from them. Some birds
eat the chemicals. When they lay eggs the shells
are very weak. They break before the baby birds
hatch. Some kinds of birds are becoming rare.

Sometimes the chemicals run off the land
into streams. They poison the fish.

Fish killed by
pollution

Snow leopards have
beautiful fur.
Hunters kill them
for it. Now there
are only a few left

Poison from industry

Many factories empty chemicals into rivers. They kill fish and plants. The polluted water flows into the sea. It kills the fish and plants that live there as well.

Sometimes oil leaks into the sea from giant oil tankers. Sea birds become covered with the oil. They cannot fly or feed. Some birds may be rescued and cleaned. But most die.

A tanker accident

Birds covered in oil

Wildlife in the
Everglades

Protecting wildlife

In many countries, land has been used to protect animals and plants in their natural homes. This land is called a wildlife reserve. The Everglades are a wildlife reserve in the United States. People can see alligators and white ibis birds there.

Making the air clean

New laws have been passed to stop air pollution. Cars must be checked to make sure they do not pollute the air.

Checking cars to prevent air pollution

A new town

Building better cities

Many people are tired of the
noise and dirt of cities. They
would like to move to new
towns in the countryside. In
these towns there are plenty of
trees and gardens. There is
space for children to play in
safety away from the roads and
cars. There are modern houses.
And people do not have to
travel far to spend a sunny day
in the countryside.

But not everyone can have a house and garden in a new town.
Ways will have to be found to make our cities better. New
houses will have to be built in place of the slums. New kinds
of energy will have to be found to keep the cities running.

People have many problems to solve. But the Earth still has
a lot to offer. Today people are beginning to use it more wisely.
So in the future the Earth might be an even better place to live.

Index

Acknowledgements

The author and publishers gratefully acknowledge the help given by the National Aeronautics and Space Administration in supplying the photographs used on pages 15 and 17.

Grateful acknowledgement is also made to Tudor Art Agency Ltd. for their assistance in the preparation of the artwork illustrations for this book.